For Mark,
with warm regards,

Michael Byers

WHO OWNS THE ARCTIC?

UNDERSTANDING

SOVEREIGNTY DISPUTES

in THE NORTH

MICHAEL BYERS

Douglas & McIntyre
D&M PUBLISHERS INC.
Vancouver/Toronto/Berkeley

Douglas & McIntyre
An imprint of D&M Publishers Inc.
2323 Quebec Street, Suite 201
Vancouver BC Canada V5T 4S7
www.douglas-mcintyre.com

Library and Archives Canada Cataloguing in Publication

Byers, Michael, 1966–
Who owns the Arctic? : understanding sovereignty disputes in the north / Michael Byers.

Includes index.
ISBN 978-1-55365-499-5

1. Arctic regions—International status. 2. Arctic regions—
International cooperation. 3. Canada—Boundaries—Arctic regions.
4. Arctic regions—Boundaries—Canada. 5. Jurisdiction, Territorial—
Arctic regions. 6. Environmental protection—Arctic regions. I. Title.

FC191.B93 2009   341.4'209719   C2009-904549-4

Editing by Barbara Pulling
Cover and text design by Ingrid Paulson
Cover photographs by iStock and Janis Christie/Getty Images
Maps on pages 23, 99 and 106 are from "Canada's Unresolved Maritime Boundaries"
by David H. Gray, *IBRU Boundary and Security Bulletin*, Autumn 1997. Used with permission.
Maps on pages 2, 31 and 37 by Paul Edmunds.
Printed and bound in Canada by Friesens
Printed on acid-free paper that is forest friendly (100% post-consumer
recycled paper) and has been processed chlorine free
Distributed in the U.S. by Publishers Group West

We gratefully acknowledge the financial support of the Canada Council for the Arts,
the British Columbia Arts Council, the Province of British Columbia through
the Book Publishing Tax Credit and the Government of Canada through the Book
Publishing Industry Development Program (BPIDP) for our publishing activities.

Mixed Sources
Cert no. SW-COC-001271
© 1996 FSC
FSC

Contents

Acknowledgements

MY FIRST CHILDHOOD memory is of my father, a federal government scientist, returning from an expedition to Polar Bear Pass on Bathurst Island with a new, very bushy beard. That memory is partly responsible for my passion for the North. I thank Bob Byers for that, and for having read and commented on every page in this book.

I am also grateful to Suzanne Lalonde of the Université de Montréal. We have sailed the Northwest Passage, debated all the legal technicalities of that waterway, and co-authored several articles. In one sense, she is the co-author of this book, too, for she has profoundly influenced my thinking.

A number of other friends and colleagues have provided much valued input on different sections of the manuscript: David Gray, formerly of the Canadian Hydrographic Service; Rob Huebert of the University of Calgary; Ron Macnab, formerly of the Canadian Geological Survey and Canadian Polar Commission; James Manicom of the University of Toronto; Ted McDorman of the University of Victoria; Don McRae of the University of Ottawa; and Justin Nankivell of the Asia-Pacific Center for Security Studies in Honolulu.

Tony Penikett, the former premier of the Yukon Territory and chief devolution negotiator for the Government of Nunavut, has been generous with his time. So too has Thomas Berger, retired judge, commissioner in the Mackenzie Valley Pipeline Inquiry and conciliator in the ongoing dispute over the implementation of the Nunavut Land Claims Agreement Act.

Travelling in the Arctic is expensive and logistically challenging. I am grateful to Bill Rompkey and his colleagues on the Standing Senate Committee on Fisheries and Oceans for taking me on their tour of Nunavut in 2008. I am also grateful to Jack Layton, the leader of the federal New Democratic Party, who took me on his northern tour the previous year.

My research has been greatly facilitated by two grants from ArcticNet, a federally funded consortium of scientists from twenty-seven Canadian universities and five federal departments. Thanks to ArcticNet, I was able to spend eleven days on the Canadian Coast Guard research icebreaker *Amundsen* during its historic late-season voyage through the Northwest Passage in October 2006. Louis Fortier and Martin Fortier, the research and executive directors of ArcticNet, have my deepest thanks.

Many Inuit shared their experience and insights. They include John Amagoalik, the "Father of Nunavut"; Paul Kaludjak, the president of Nunavut Tunngavik Inc.; Letia Obed, the director of Aboriginal and Circumpolar Affairs for the Government of Nunavut; Paul Okalik, the former premier of Nunavut; Aaju Peter, lawyer, artist, cultural interpreter; Mary Simon, the president of Inuit Tapiriit Kanatami; and Sheila Watt-Cloutier, former president of the Inuit Circumpolar Council. ᖁᔭᓐᓇᒦᒃ (Naqurmiik). Thank you.

Other northerners also deserve my thanks: Joe Ballantyne, former Federal Land Use Administrator for Canada's Arctic islands; Dennis Bevington, Member of Parliament for the Northwest Territories; Paul Crowley and Lynn Peplinski of Iqaluit; Ben McDonald and Craig Yeo of Alternatives North in Yellowknife; Mark Salvor, devolution negotiator for the Government of the

Northwest Territories; Clint Sawicki of the Northern Research Institute at Yukon College in Whitehorse; Shelley Wright, former northern director of the Akitsiraq Law School in Iqaluit; and Arthur Yuan, legal adviser to Nunavut Tunngavik Inc.

I am indebted to Donat Pharand and Franklyn Griffiths, retired professors at the universities of Ottawa and Toronto, respectively, for their extensive writings on the law and politics of Arctic sovereignty.

Arctic consultant Terry Fenge has been a reliable source of information and inspiration, as has Colonel (retired) Pierre Leblanc, former commander of Canadian Forces Northern Area. Two of Colonel Leblanc's successors, Colonel Norm Couturier and Brigadier-General Christine Whitecross, kindly invited me to sit in on the all-important biannual meetings of the Arctic Security Working Group.

Captain Alain Gariépy shared his vast knowledge of Arctic navigation during long nights on the bridge of the *Amundsen*, while Vice Admiral D.W. Robertson invited me to take part in an Arctic sovereignty simulation at Canadian Forces Base Halifax. Jacob Verhoef, the director of the Atlantic division of the Geological Survey of Canada, gave me a good grounding in seabed mapping. David Hik, the executive director of the Canadian International Polar Year Secretariat, invited me to give the speech that became the skeleton of this book.

Many American colleagues have also been helpful. Paul Cellucci, the former U.S. ambassador to Canada, partnered with me in a model Canada-U.S. negotiation on northern waters. Ashley Roach, formerly of the Office of the Legal Adviser, U.S. State Department, responded positively to a request to meet with him and his colleagues in Washington, D.C. George Newton, the former chair of the U.S. Arctic Research Commission and a former U.S. nuclear submariner, was generous with his insights. Diddy Hitchens of the University of Alaska, Christopher Joyner of Georgetown University and Doug Nord of Western Washington University have opened doors, organized events and supported grant applications.

Poul Erik Dam Kristensen, the former Danish ambassador to Canada, has been a valued interlocutor, as has Evgeny Avdoshin of the Russian Embassy. Mark Entin of the Moscow State Institute of International Relations, Geir Ulfstein of the University of Oslo, Colin Warbrick of the University of Birmingham, Nicholas Wheeler of the University of Wales, Aberystwyth, and three Berlin-based colleagues—Heike Krieger of the Free University, Georg Nolte of Humboldt University and Michael Zürn of the Hertie School of Governance—provided support, constructive criticism and groups of students on whom to test ideas.

Herb Gray, former deputy prime minister and Canadian chair of the International Joint Commission, graciously provided the perfect venue for the model Canada-U.S. negotiation, while Michael Vechsler, the IJC's legal counsel, handled the arrangements with aplomb.

I owe a particular debt to the 130 students who took my course "Arctic Sovereignty and International Relations" at the University of British Columbia in early 2009, as well as to my teaching assistants Matt Lesch and Jan Luedert. Our classroom discussions coincided with, and substantially influenced, the writing of this book.

My research has been facilitated by the expert journalism of Patricia Bell of CBC North, Randy Boswell of the *Ottawa Citizen*, Bob Weber of the Canadian Press and Chris Windeyer of the *Nunatsiaq News*. I am also grateful to Doug Struck of the *Washington Post*, who shared a cabin with me on the *Amundsen*, as well as his incredible photographs of our voyage. I look at them often, and every time I do so, they take me back—to a wild and beautiful place that is part of my country's soul.

Introduction

Are the Russians Coming?

TWO TUPOLEV TU-95 bombers took off from Engels Air Base in southern Russia on February 18, 2009. They turned north and flew on a straight course for almost ten hours. The route carried them over the Barents Sea, past Norway's Svalbard Islands, across the geographic North Pole, then south toward the Beaufort Sea.

The "Bears," as these long-range, high-altitude turboprop planes are popularly called, would have been spotted by the North Atlantic Treaty Organization (NATO) before they reached the Pole. The U.S. military has a powerful new radar facility at Thule Air Base in northern Greenland, while the joint U.S.-Canada North American Aerospace Defense Command (NORAD) operates a string of radar stations across the High Arctic—an upgraded version of the old DEW Line.

Two CF-18 fighter-interceptors were scrambled out of Canadian Forces Base Cold Lake in northern Alberta. They met up with the Russian planes over the Beaufort Sea, some 200 km north of the mouth of the Mackenzie River. In accordance with long-standing practice, the Russian and Canadian pilots would have waved at each other and then turned their planes around. The Russian planes were nowhere near Canadian airspace, which,

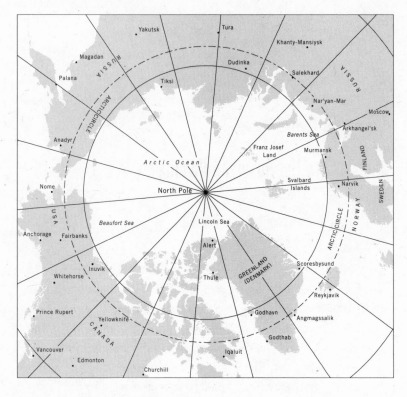

The Circumpolar Arctic / SOURCE: PAUL EDMUNDS

under international law, extends just 12 nautical miles (22 km) from shore.

In a sharp departure from routine, the encounter was revealed to the press nine days later. Canadian Defence Minister Peter Mac-Kay pointed out that the incident had occurred just one day before U.S. President Barack Obama visited Ottawa, and then stated: "I am not going to stand here and accuse the Russians of having deliberately done this during the presidential visit, but it was a strong coincidence."

Later, when Prime Minister Stephen Harper was asked about the matter, he suggested that the Russian planes had actually entered Canadian airspace. "This is a real concern to us," he said. "I have expressed at various times the deep concern our government has with increasingly aggressive Russian actions around the globe and Russian intrusions into our airspace." Harper promised to "respond every time the Russians make any kind of intrusion on the sovereignty of Canada's Arctic."

The inaccurate accusations were clearly not appreciated by the United States. NORAD commander Gene Renuart took the unusual step of publicly correcting the Canadian ministers. The four-star U.S. general told journalists: "The Russians have conducted themselves professionally; they have maintained compliance with the international rules of airspace sovereignty and have not entered the internal airspace of either of the countries."

National Post columnist Don Martin cuttingly described the situation as "Peter MacKay's Dr. Strangelove moment," a reference to the 1964 movie about a crazed American general who starts a nuclear war. Martin dismissed the suggestion that the Russian flights might have been timed to coincide with Obama's visit: "Let the record show that Ottawa is about 5,000 kilometres southwest [*sic*] of our Arctic air space boundary. Those ancient lumbering bombers would've taken at least five hours to reach Ottawa at top speed, which is about 4 hours and 57 minutes longer than they would've stayed aloft if their mission was perceived as hostile."

The Russian government too was concerned about MacKay's and Harper's comments: concerned enough that Defence Minister Anatoliy Serdyukov took the unusual step of publishing an op-ed article in the *National Post*. Serdyukov wrote that the "aggressive tone" taken by Canada was "worrisome, not because there is any possibility of reigniting a cold war between our two great nations, but because it placed an unnecessary and counterproductive strain on our good relationship." He pointed out that Canada's principal Arctic disputes are with the United States and Denmark and accused Stephen Harper and Peter MacKay of practising the "ages-old political tactic of misdirection" under "the guise of protecting Canada's Arctic territorial claims."

Serdyukov also expressed the hope that "as the Canadian government presses its Arctic claims it will address the real issues related to those claims rather than misdirecting the Canadian public." A similar sentiment was concurrently expressed by four Canadian historians and political scientists. In their book *Arctic Front*, Ken Coates, Whitney Lackenbauer, William Morrison and Greg Poelzer wrote:

> An Arctic strategy based on current headlines will not work. Today's threats relate to boundaries and resources. Tomorrow, environmental considerations will likely dominate the news, followed by accounts of further difficulties in indigenous communities. Canada and the Canadian government need to step back from the rhetoric of militarization and strategic approaches to the Arctic. The Far North is not going anywhere, the Russians aren't coming, and the real threats to Canadian sovereignty are much less dramatic than current rhetoric would have the country believe.

I agree entirely, albeit from the slightly different perspective of an international lawyer. This short book is my contribution to helping Canadians understand the highly charged issue of Arctic sovereignty and the complex interface between international law and politics it involves. There is, it turns out, a great deal of international cooperation taking place, including between Canada and Russia. And there is a major opportunity—which has not yet been seized—for Canada to lead in the creation of a truly cooperative, permanently peaceful North.

Chapter One

Why Sovereignty Matters

SOVEREIGNTY 101

Thomas Hobbes's *Leviathan* is required reading for political science students. I still remember the cover of my first copy, which featured the portrait of a supremely confident-looking king under the Latin inscription *Non est potestas Super Terram quae Comparetur ei* ("There is no power on earth that can be compared with him").

Sovereignty means different things to different people. Sovereignty can be about power, authority, autonomy, identity or moral equivalence. For international lawyers, sovereignty is the totality of different forms of exclusive jurisdiction exercised by a state within its boundaries. From this perspective, sovereignty is closely related to statehood, which was famously defined in the 1933 Montevideo Convention on the Rights and Duties of States as requiring: (a) a permanent population; (b) defined territory; (c) government; and (d) capacity to enter into relations with other states.

Canada's Arctic disputes do not involve our country's status as a sovereign state. They concern the precise limits of Canadian territory and the possibility that international law might limit Canada's rights within parts of that territory or accord Canada some rights adjacent to that territory.

Take Hans Island. Canada and Denmark's conflicting claims over the small outcrop of rock between Ellesmere Island and Greenland constitute a straightforward territorial dispute over the geographic extent of sovereignty. Whichever country prevails will rightfully control who visits Hans Island and what they do there. That country could also choose to sell the island, like Russia sold Alaska to the United States in 1867. It could give the island away, like Britain did when it assigned the North American Arctic Archipelago (sans Greenland) to Canada in 1880. It could lease it out, like Cuba leased Guantánamo Bay to the United States in 1903. It could mine the island, settle it, blow it up or leave it alone. It could even declare the island a condominium and share it with another country.

With the exception of a few island-states, most sovereign territory abuts the sovereign territory of at least one other country. The places where territories meet are "borders" on land and "boundaries" at sea. Boundaries also exist between areas subject to sovereign rights rather than full sovereignty, such as between the continental shelves of adjoining or opposing coastal states. Sometimes countries disagree on the location of a border or boundary and, therefore, the geographic extent of their respective sovereignties. Canada has no disputed land borders, but it does have a number of maritime boundary disputes, including two in the Arctic. One of these, only 220 km² in total size, concerns the boundary between Canada and Denmark (that is, Greenland, an island Denmark owns) in the Lincoln Sea. The other, more significant dispute is with the United States over 21,436 km² in the Beaufort Sea.

Sovereignty, like property, can usefully be thought of as a bundle of rights. A homeowner is still a homeowner if her property is subject to an easement entitling a neighbour to share a driveway, or to a covenant that prohibits the removal of trees. In the same way, if the Northwest Passage were considered an "international strait," rather than "internal waters," Canada would retain ownership of the waterway. One strand of our sovereignty would be lost, however: the ability to exercise full control over foreign ships passing through.

No country will ever "own" the North Pole, which is located roughly 750 km to the north of any land, including Ellesmere Island, Greenland and the Russian archipelago of Franz Josef Land. This is because coastal states cannot possess full sovereignty more than 12 nautical miles (22 km) from shore. Instead, they have certain "sovereignty rights" out to 200 nautical miles (370 km) and sometimes farther, depending on the shape and sediments of the seabed. If Canada, Denmark or Russia can scientifically demonstrate that the North Pole is a "natural prolongation" of its continental shelf, the country in question will have the exclusive right to exploit the resources of the seabed there—and nothing more. The water and sea-ice will remain part of the "high seas," meaning that ships and planes will be able to travel freely, and tourists and adventurers from anywhere in the world will be able to visit without producing passports or paying fees.

The North Pole is just one point in an ocean that is thousands of kilometres across. There might be some symbolic nationalistic value in scientifically proving the existence of sovereign rights at the globe's northern axis, but the same exercise still has to be repeated at every other location in the Arctic where such rights are claimed. Regardless of what happens at the Pole, Canada will end up with recognized sovereign rights over a very large expanse of the Arctic Ocean floor.

Sovereignty is related to self-determination, which is the right of a people to freely determine their political status. Recognized in the 1945 UN Charter, self-determination was an important factor in the decolonization of the developing world. But it remains unsettled as to whether, and in what circumstances, self-determination entitles a people to carve a new state out of a territorially cohesive pre-existing country. Think of Kosovo, Kurdistan, or indeed Quebec.

Canada's Inuit are not seeking independence, but they believe their right of self-determination entitles them to participate in decision-making about the North. In April 2009, they joined with the Inuit of Alaska, Greenland and Russia in issuing "A Circumpolar Inuit Declaration on Sovereignty in the Arctic." The document makes a strong case for Inuit involvement in any interstate negotiations concerning sovereignty disputes. The case is all the more compelling because the Inuit have already exercised self-determination in a manner that strengthens Canadian sovereignty: they transferred a claim to aboriginal title over one-fifth of Canadian territory by concluding the 1993 Nunavut Land Claims Agreement. In doing so, they explicitly assigned to Canada any sovereign rights that the Inuit and their ancestors had acquired through thousands of years of use and occupancy of both land and sea-ice.

A CHANGING ARCTIC

In today's Arctic, sovereignty matters because of climate change, which is more apparent there than anywhere else on earth. Some of the change is being driven by "feedback loops" that arise out of the precarious balance between water and ice. An increase in average annual temperature of just a fraction of one degree can transform a large expanse of highly reflective sea-ice into dark, heat-absorbing ocean water. It can also turn rock-hard, chemically stable permafrost into a decomposing, methane-emitting morass of ancient plant material. In the last four decades, average annual temperatures in Alaska, the Northwest Territories and western Nunavut have increased by around 3° Celsius.

Climate change is altering the North at astonishing speed. When I visited Auyuittuq National Park in August 2007, park manager David Argument pointed to rapidly retreating glaciers, melting permafrost and strikingly green tundra. Ironically, in a park whose Inuktitut name means "land that never melts," dozens of hikers were evacuated the following summer when high temperatures created an extreme risk of flash floods.

In nearby Pangnirtung, Mayor Manasa Evic explained that the caribou have all but disappeared, while rising ocean temperatures have caused the collapse of a multimillion-dollar commercial ice fishery. Canada's northernmost community, Grise Fiord, lost its regular water supply after the source glacier melted away; the intrepid residents have been chopping up icebergs instead. While on board the Coast Guard research icebreaker *Amundsen* in late October 2006, I witnessed the absence of sea-ice in the Northwest Passage—and saw just how easy it would be for cargo ships to sail through.

In an increasingly accessible Arctic, much depends on Canada having clearly defined boundaries and the undisputed authority to apply its laws within them. The alternative is a Wild West situation, where might makes right and the vulnerable—including the environment and northern residents—suffer.

In the nineteenth century, Canada avoided general lawlessness on its western frontier by deploying the North West Mounted Police in advance of the settlers. Our ability to manage expansion in a mostly peaceful manner contributed to our distinctiveness from the United States, where the frontier was a chaotic and dangerous place. Today, we face similar challenges and opportunities in the Arctic. Securing clarity as to the extent of our sovereign rights, and developing the capacity to assert and protect them, is a national project for the twenty-first century.

OIL AND GAS

Sovereignty matters because of natural resources as well. In May 2009, the U.S. Geological Survey released some truly stunning projections of undiscovered oil and gas resources north of the Arctic

Circle: 83 billion barrels of oil, which is enough to meet current global demands for three years; and 44 trillion cubic metres of natural gas, or about fourteen years' worth of supply. With most of the projected reserves located in waters less than 500 metres deep, the resources will likely fall within the uncontested jurisdiction of one or another Arctic Ocean coastal state.

Until recently, vast distances, winter darkness, inclement weather and ever-present thick and moving sea-ice made it prohibitively expensive to access Arctic oil and gas. But increased market prices and climate change have altered the situation. Gazprom is spending $20 billion developing the Shtokman field in the Russian portion of the Barents Sea, which is estimated to hold 3.8 trillion cubic metres of natural gas. On the Norwegian side, the smaller but still sizeable Snøhvit field is already producing. Exxon and BP recently spent $585 million and $1.2 billion respectively to acquire exploration licences on the Canadian side of the Beaufort Sea.

So far, concerns about the security of drilling licences have discouraged oil and gas exploration in areas of disputed sovereignty. But Big Oil, which is willing to deal with just about any government, is starting to push for agreed-upon boundaries. Governments, realizing that clear jurisdiction is a prerequisite for large-scale investment, are beginning to respond. Russia and Norway have negotiated a solution for the south Barents Sea; they are now working on their disputed boundary farther north. In May 2008, Denmark hosted a summit in Greenland at which the five Arctic Ocean countries reaffirmed their commitment to the law of the sea—including an existing scientific mechanism for vetting claims to extended continental shelves. Oil company executives no doubt breathed a collective sigh of relief.

In addition to preventing conflict between countries and providing stability for oil companies, using international law to delimit Arctic boundaries might serve another, less obvious function. We must never lose sight of the fact that the very opportunity to access

Arctic oil and gas has arisen because we have burned so much oil and gas already and, by doing so, begun to change the climate. Ultimately, establishing clear boundaries may enable responsible governments to ensure that the carbon stays locked in the seabed, where it cannot contribute to even more ever more dangerous climate change.

SHIPPING

Increased amounts of shipping in the Arctic, related to both industry and tourism, are also making sovereignty more important than before. Although Canada has the longest coastline of any country, most of it is in the Arctic, and our northern coastline had for centuries been rendered inaccessible by thick, hard "multi-year" sea-ice, formed when ice survives one or more summers and new ice accretes to it. Now, climate change is causing the ice to disappear. The minimal summer extent of sea-ice was down 1 million km^2 between September 2006 and September 2007, opening the Northwest Passage temporarily. The waterway was free of ice again in September 2008.

Soon, all of the Arctic's sea-ice will melt away during the summer months. From that point onward, a great deal of ice will still form during winter, but it will be relatively thin, soft "first-year" ice—not the multi-year ice that poses the principal hazard to shipping. Regular cargo ships will be able to operate throughout the year with icebreaker assistance, while purpose-built ice-strengthened vessels will be able to travel alone. Hundreds of such ships are already being built in Finland and South Korea, many of them dual-direction vessels that will sail normally and efficiently in open water, then turn round and use their propellers—like Weed Eaters—to chew their way through first-year ice.

Since the earth is a sphere, Canada's northern coastline is relatively close to both Asia and Europe. The Northwest Passage offers a 7,000-kilometre shortcut between East Asia and the Atlantic

Seaboard, as compared with the usual route through the Panama Canal. Sailing straight across the Arctic Ocean would cut the distance from East Asia to Europe in half, while avoiding the crowded and pirate-infested Strait of Malacca. Shipping to and from northern Russia and Canada has already increased, with more to come as shorter, warmer winters curtail the use of seasonal roads over frozen lakes and tundra, and melting permafrost causes pipelines to heave and crack.

More than 150 cruise ships sail along the coast of Greenland each summer. Dozens more enter the Canadian Arctic Archipelago, while a few visit the North Pole. Search-and-rescue officials in Denmark and Canada are concerned because these are remote, incompletely charted and sometimes stormy waters. Icebergs are also becoming more common, as water produced by the melting of Greenland's glaciers lubricates the underlying rock and accelerates their movement into the sea. In November 2007, a Canadian-owned cruise ship struck a small "growler" off Antarctica and sank; fortunately for the mostly elderly passengers, the weather was good and other ships were nearby. The vessel that sank had been a frequent visitor to northern waters. Adventurers are also heading north in growing numbers. Each summer now, private yachts attempt the Northwest Passage, giving their owners bragging rights back home—and sometimes necessitating long-range search-and-rescue operations that cost Canadian taxpayers dearly.

The increased activity by ships in the Arctic poses risks to fragile, already precarious ecosystems—risks that can adequately be addressed only through the application and enforcement of Canada's shipping safety and environmental laws.

ENVIRONMENTAL PROTECTION

Many Arctic species have evolved specifically for life under or on the now-disappearing sea-ice. Unique forms of algae and bacteria are active below and within cracks in the ice at temperatures as low as minus 22° Celsius. They are fed upon by minute crustaceans, which, in turn, are consumed by Arctic cod, a species of fish that has antifreeze proteins in its blood. The cod are preyed upon by ringed seals, which give birth and nurse their pups in dens inside sea-ice ridges. The seals are the main food source for polar bears, a species perfectly adapted to find and kill seals in the whiteness—and, in winter, total darkness—of the frozen sea.

The risks posed to these species are reflected in the U.S. government's decision to list the polar bear as threatened, a move that blocks American big game hunters from taking trophies home from northern Canada. The Inuit scorn the decision. In Resolute Bay, where elders recall hunting the formidable creatures with spears, scores of three-metre-long skins are tacked on the sides of houses to dry. The bears are in trouble 2,000 km to the south, but where the populations remain healthy, the Inuit still hunt them, or guide foreigners who pay handsomely for the privilege. The continued hunting does not result from a lack of awareness about the species' long-term prospects; it is just that the Inuit regard the protections as hypocritical and ineffective. And they are right, since the root of the problem is climate change, which is driven primarily by greenhouse gas emissions in the South.

The Inuit are themselves at threat from climate change. When my colleague Suzanne Lalonde and I asked Maria Kripanik, the deputy mayor of Igloolik, about the likelihood of increased shipping through the Northwest Passage, her first thought was for "our animals." The waters of Foxe Basin, she explained, are home to belugas, ringed seals and walrus, which the Inuit still depend on for much of their food. The Inuit are a maritime people, as is reflected in the fact that all but one of Nunavut's communities are on the seacoast; the exception, Baker Lake, is located beside a large body of fresh water.

Within three generations, the Inuit have undergone a sharp transition from igloos to houses, dog teams to airplanes, and story-telling to TV and the Internet—at enormous social cost. The suicide rate among the Inuit is eleven times the Canadian average, with most of the victims being directionless young men who, just a few decades ago, would have been providing for their families "on the land." The melting ice has become part of the problem, sometimes stranding those who still venture out and even claiming their lives as they plunge through thin and weakened patches. Across the Arctic, Inuit hunters striving to maintain their independence and cultural identity are paying the ultimate price.

From the bacteria underneath the ice to the people above, food chains in the Arctic are short, highly specialized and easily disrupted. Oil poses a particular threat, since it disperses and degrades very slowly at cold temperatures. As a point of comparison, the worst oil spill in history, that of the *Exxon Valdez*, took place in the relatively warm, ice-free waters off southern Alaska. The remoteness of Canada's Arctic Archipelago would make cleanup efforts even more expensive and time-consuming, as well as largely ineffective.

The legal dispute over the status of the Northwest Passage exacerbates the risk. An oil tanker that does not meet Canada's Arctic shipping standards might decide against requesting permission for passage. As a result, it might not have the latest information about ice, weather and navigation hazards. The Canadian Coast Guard might not be aware of the ship's presence, thus slowing the agency's response to any spill.

Already, each summer, one or more foreign cruise ships fails to register before entering Canada's Arctic waters. Although these vessels are attracted by the beauty of the Arctic, they pose environmental risks. In Pangnirtung, Inuit hunters worry that eco-cruises will be drawn to the local beluga nursery in Clearwater Fiord, an area the Inuit for centuries have carefully avoided during the summer birthing season.

The range of interests engaged by our changing Arctic makes it difficult for governments to agree on safeguards. The London-based International Maritime Organization spent years developing a mandatory Arctic Code for shipping in northern waters, but the document was downgraded to a set of guidelines before it was submitted to the member states in 2001. The membership of the IMO includes both shipping states seeking maximum freedom of navigation and smaller island and coastal states primarily intent on protecting the environment along their shores.

Much like people who never wash the cars they rent, those who do not own part of the Arctic have little incentive to accept restrictions on access. Mandatory controls are more likely to come through national legislation, which is one reason Canada is adamant that the Northwest Passage constitute internal waters rather than an international strait. As Professor Rob Huebert of the University of Calgary has explained, "The IMO may, ultimately, create a set of standards equal to those developed in Canada; but, more likely, an internationally established set of standards would not be as stringent on such issues as environmental protection."

In April 2009, the Arctic Council released the Arctic Marine Shipping Assessment, a 194-page overview of the challenges resulting from increased shipping in the Circumpolar North. Prominent among those challenges are the risks posed to the environment, which the assessment identifies as follows:

> The most significant threat from ships to the Arctic marine environment is the release of oil through accidental or illegal discharge. Additional potential impacts of Arctic ships include ship strikes on marine mammals, the introduction of alien species, disruption of migratory patterns of marine mammals and anthropogenic noise produced from marine shipping activity.

Unfortunately, the assessment's recommendations with respect to law-making are quite limited. The document encourages Arctic Council member-states to liaise with international organizations, promote the development and mandatory application of currently voluntary International Maritime Organization guidelines and harmonize domestic safety shipping regimes. It does make one more significant and valuable recommendation: to develop and implement "a comprehensive, multi-national Arctic Search and Rescue (SAR) instrument, including aeronautical and maritime SAR, among the eight Arctic nations."

Multilateral treaties sometimes take decades to negotiate and decades more to attract sufficient ratifications to bring them into force. With millions of square kilometres of sea-ice disappearing, that is time we do not have. As I will argue in Chapter 5, our best shot at protecting the environment and the Inuit in the Northwest Passage involves persuading the United States to accept Canada's unlimited sovereignty there.

SECURITY

International security threats have changed dramatically since the end of the Cold War and the September 11, 2001, terrorist attacks on New York and Washington, and this situation has made Arctic sovereignty more crucial.

The enormity and remoteness of the Arctic did not isolate it from the Cold War, when the Soviet Union, the United States and their allies built runways, radar stations and underwater acoustic devices for detecting submarines. But today, it is important to remember that the North Pole is closer to Paris than it is to Ottawa. Russia's northernmost possession, the archipelago of Franz Josef Land, is more than 1,500 km away from Canada's Ellesmere Island. In the changed security landscape of the early twenty-first century, the most significant threats in the Arctic are found along its southern fringes, in places like Baffin Bay, the Beaufort Sea and the Northwest Passage. These threats involve non-state actors rather than other nation-states.

Former U.S. ambassador Paul Cellucci has expressed concern about the risk that terrorist groups might use the Northwest Passage to traffic in weapons of mass destruction. An ice-free Northwest Passage could also serve as an entry point for drugs, guns and illegal immigrants. Gravel airstrips are scattered along the waterway, a forgotten legacy of the Cold War and countless research and prospecting expeditions. Each summer, cruise ships put hundreds of undocumented foreign nationals on shore in Inuit communities with scheduled air service but no immigration controls.

Stories about attempts at illegal immigration abound in Canada's Arctic. In September 2006, a Romanian man was deported from Canada after overstaying his student visa. Desperate to return to his Canadian girlfriend in Toronto, the young man flew to Thule, Greenland, bought a six-metre fibreglass motorboat and set out for Ellesmere Island. Miraculously, he made it across Baffin Bay to the tiny hamlet of Grise Fiord, where scheduled flights would have taken him to Iqaluit, Ottawa and ultimately back to Toronto. But news travels fast in communities of only two hundred people, and he was soon facing questions from the local RCMP.

The next month, two Turkish sailors jumped ship at Churchill, Manitoba, and bought train tickets to Winnipeg. They too were arrested by the RCMP, after the VIA Rail ticket agent became suspicious about their ignorance of Canadian geography.

In August 2007, Michelle Gillis gave me a lift into Cambridge Bay from the hamlet's small airport. As she drove into town, the young mayor told me that local RCMP officers had just arrested five Norwegian adventurers intent on challenging Canada's Northwest Passage claim. The self-designated "Vikings"—complete with horned helmets—had sailed their yacht, the *Berserk II*, three-quarters of the way through the Passage without seeking permission. However, the Norwegians had a history. During a stop in Halifax, two of them had been involved in a barroom brawl, arrested and deported from Canada after a computer search revealed they were members of the Norwegian branch of the Hells Angels motorcycle gang. The two men rejoined their vessel in Greenland, and, when their compatriots stopped in Cambridge Bay to do some shopping, they went ashore outside the town.

Fortunately, they were detected. Because the two men had violated the terms of their deportations by setting foot on indisputably sovereign Canadian soil, the status of the Northwest Passage no longer mattered. The RCMP intervened, assisted by the Canadian Coast Guard icebreaker *Sir Wilfrid Laurier*. This time all five Norwegians were deported. It was a humorous incident that could easily have been more serious. What if, instead of a small yacht, the vessel had been a single-hulled oil tanker flying a flag of convenience, or a container ship with possible links to al Qaeda, North Korea or Iran? On the positive side, the *Berserk II* incident demonstrated that civilian authorities are fully capable of upholding Canadian laws in the Northwest Passage if they have the appropriate equipment and political support. In this instance, a twenty-one-year-old light icebreaker was up to the task, while some quiet diplomacy prevented an official Norwegian protest.

Unfortunately, Stephen Harper's government has focussed almost exclusively on military solutions to Arctic security challenges. Canada's older, heavier Coast Guard icebreakers are at the end of their lifespan, but instead of replacements the prime minister has promised six to eight ice-strengthened patrol ships for the navy. Although Harper later announced plans for one new Coast Guard icebreaker, no steps have been taken to build or acquire the vessel.

As we will see in Chapter 4, naval vessels are not suitable for dealing with the threats associated with international shipping, which range from illegal immigrants to oil spills. Nor are they able to fulfill the other roles played by Coast Guard icebreakers, from maintaining navigation aids to supporting Arctic research.

Glenn Gould called it the "Idea of North"; Professor Franklyn Griffiths of the University of Toronto termed it the "Arctic sublime." Canadians inherited a fascination with the Arctic from the British, for whom polar exploration—and especially the quest for the Northwest Passage—was a national project for centuries. We have since made it our own, through the quintessentially Canadian literature, art and music of Robert Service, Farley Mowat, Zacharias Kunuk, Kenojuak Ashevak, Susan Aglukark and many others.

Hundreds of thousands of Canadians have lived and worked in the North. Jean-Guy Quenneville, who taught me international relations at the University of Saskatchewan, worked as an electrician on the DEW Line during the Cold War. Ever since, a magnificent polar bear skin has covered most of a wall in his house. Others worked for oil and mining companies exploring for riches and, from places like Nanisivik and Bent Horn, sending some of it south. Many others worked as civil servants: regulating and policing all the activity; breaking ice; building and maintaining runways; providing search-and-rescue, health, education and social services; or—like my own father did in 1969—conducting scientific research.

After every speech I give about the Arctic, from Victoria to Halifax, at least one audience member comes up to me to reveal a connection with the North. It is a personal, even emotional experience, because the Arctic gets into our hearts and minds and becomes part of who we are. Because so many of us have these connections, the Arctic is part of our national psyche, too. The northern dimension of our identity is strengthened by the familiarity that most Canadians have with Arctic weather. I have vivid memories of walking home from classes at the University of Saskatchewan at minus 40°, with the snow crunching under my feet and the aurora borealis playing across the sky. In most of Canada, Arctic conditions are—for two or three months each year—a regular fact of life.

Paradoxically, our northern sensibility is present in spite of the fact that most Canadians have no direct stake in the Arctic. Although Canada's Arctic extends from the Atlantic Ocean in northern Labrador to within 100 km of the Pacific Ocean in the southern Yukon, only 1 per cent of Canadians live there. For the rest of us, the Arctic transcends regional differences and rivalries. It is the most irritant-free part of our national identity, this "True North Strong and Free."

Conceptions of sovereignty are often wrapped up in national identities, and nowhere is this more true than with Canada's North. For many Canadians, when the United States claims an unfettered right to use the Northwest Passage, it is like a wealthy neighbour claiming the right to tramp through our living room. Simply put, it offends our sense of self.

As Franklyn Griffiths elegantly explained in 1985:

> [N]otions about the Northwest Passage, and the Arctic, are lodged deep in Canadians' conceptions of themselves as a people. Those who would diminish Canada's Arctic presence by challenging our legal position in the Passage would take away some of our self-regard and distinctiveness. The Canadian Government that presided over a loss of jurisdiction in the Passage would have much to answer for. The United States should understand this.

Politicians have long recognized the unique place the Arctic occupies in our hearts and minds. In 1958, John Diefenbaker won a massive majority on the basis of his "Northern Vision." In 1970, Pierre Trudeau stood up to the Americans with the Arctic Waters Pollution Prevention Act. In the 1980s, Brian Mulroney promised to build the world's largest icebreaker and to buy twelve nuclear-powered submarines that could sail under the ice. Stephen Harper has also made Arctic sovereignty part of his successful election campaigns. A deeper understanding of Arctic sovereignty could help us to discern electioneering from substantive policy-making. And it can help us get those policies right.

Finally, Arctic sovereignty matters because the North is becoming a focal point for international relations. As an Arctic country, our decisions there will define Canada's role and reputation in the world. Will we be the difficult child of international politics, dragging our heels and disrupting efforts at collaboration? Or will we exercise leadership on climate change, environmental protection, dispute settlement and NATO-Russia relations? Will we rise to the occasion? Will we become a great nation of the North?

Chapter Two

Who Owns Hans Island?

ON AN INTERNATIONAL scale, it is easy to overlook Denmark, a small Scandinavian country most often associated with LEGO and pastries. But Denmark is arguably Canada's second most important neighbour—thanks to the fact that it owns Greenland, the world's largest island.

On a clear day, northwest Greenland is visible from Canada's Ellesmere Island. Southwest Greenland is separated from Baffin Island by Baffin Bay, a body of water narrow enough that Canada and Denmark's continental shelves abut one other all the way south to the waters off Labrador. Most of this 2,685-kilometre maritime boundary is undisputed. In 1973, the two countries agreed to divide the ocean floor between Canada and Greenland down the middle, using an equidistance line defined by 127 turning points. Since then, they have used the same line to define their fishing zones, meaning that the delimitation line has informally become an all-purpose maritime boundary.

It was during the course of the 1973 negotiations that Canadian and Danish diplomats became aware of a difference of opinion concerning Hans Island, a tiny (1.3 km²) barren islet in the Kennedy Channel portion of Nares Strait between Ellesmere Island

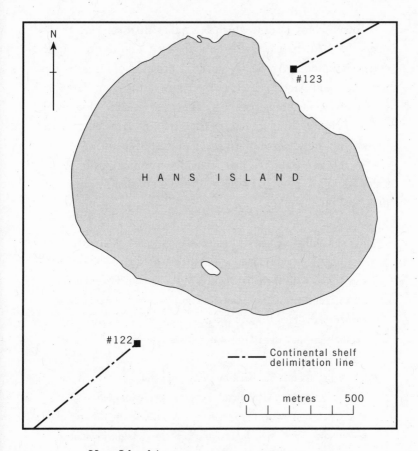

Hans Island / SOURCE: DAVID H. GRAY

and Greenland. Instead of delaying their talks with this new, almost inconsequential problem, the two countries simply drew the boundary line up to the low-water mark on one side of the island and continued it from the low-water mark on the other.

The negotiators failed to anticipate a subsequent geographic discovery. In 1975, mapping and hydrographic charting revealed that Hans Island is slightly closer to Greenland than to Canada, and the channel is deeper on the Ellesmere Island side of the island than on the Greenland side.

Today, Hans Island, which is smaller than some of the ice-bergs that drift past it, is the only disputed land territory in the entire circumpolar Arctic. Ownership of the rest of Canada's nine-teen thousand Arctic islands is uncontested, thanks in large part to Britain having transferred its claim to us in 1880. Our remain-ing sovereignty disputes concern the maritime areas between the islands and to the north, northeast and west of them.

The Danish claim to Hans Island was summarized by Ambas-sador Poul Kristensen in a letter to the editor of the *Ottawa Citizen* in 2005:

> It is generally accepted that Hans Island was first discovered in 1853 on an expedition done in agreement with the Danish authorities with the participation of the famous Greenlander Hans Hendrik of Fiskenæsset. His place in the expedition earned Hans Hendrik of Fiskenæsset a place in the history of exploration and the island was named after him—"Hans Ø" (Hans Island).
>
> Since then it has been our view that the island, by virtue of its belonging to Greenland, is part of the Kingdom of Den-mark. Relevant evidence in connection with defining the area of Greenland, such as geological and geomorphological evidence, clearly supports this point of view.
>
> In 1933, when the Permanent Court of International Justice declared the legal status of Greenland in favour of Denmark, the Court did inter alia refer to the note from the British Gov-ernment, acting on behalf of Canada, which in 1920 assured the Danish Government that it recognized Danish sovereignty over Greenland.

Another component of the argument was advanced by Tom Høyem, a former Danish minister for Greenland:

> Hans Island has been used for centuries by Greenlandic Inuit as
> an ideal vantage point to get an overview of the ice situation and
> of the hunting prospects, especially for polar bears and seals.
> The Canadian Inuit have never used the island... Hans Island is,
> in fact, an integrated part of the Thule-Inuit hunting area. They
> even gave it its local name, *Tartupaluk*, which means kidney.

However, these arguments are not terribly persuasive. Ambassador Kristensen fails to mention that Hans Hendrik was participating in an American expedition, though the United States has never claimed Hans Island. Geological and geomorphological evidence is relevant when it comes to claiming an undersea shelf more than 200 nautical miles from shore, but irrelevant with respect to an island that lies within sight of opposing coastlines. Britain's 1920 recognition of Danish title to Greenland does bind Canada, since Britain was responsible for Canada's foreign relations until 1931, but only with respect to Greenland.

The use of Hans Island by the Greenland Inuit is the only Danish argument that carries any weight, though it is not decisive. The same Inuit often travelled to Ellesmere Island, which is universally regarded as falling within Canada's sovereign control.

Canada's claim to Hans Island is based on the transfer of the North American Arctic Archipelago (excluding Greenland) from Britain in 1880. The claim also relies on "use and occupation," since international law requires that title to territory be consolidated and maintained by regular activity. Hans Island was home to a Canadian scientific base for a brief period during the Second World War. The name "Hans Island" was formally adopted by the Canadian Permanent Committee on Geographical Names in 1950. Three years later, Eric Fry of the Topographical Survey of Canada surveyed Hans Island and built a cairn, in which he left a note claiming the island for Canada. In 1972, Fry's survey point, along with survey points on Greenland, was linked by angle and distance measurements to Canada's control survey network by a Canadian government survey party that included Danish government surveyors.

The dispute "crystallized" in 1973 when the seabed boundary between Greenland and Canada was being negotiated. When an international legal dispute crystallizes, subsequent efforts by both countries to strengthen their respective positions are of no legal effect—all the more so if protests are issued. Under international law, a diplomatic protest by one country is usually sufficient to prevent the creation of sovereign rights by another country through the protested act. Notwithstanding this legal reality, the insignificant dispute over Hans Island has prompted ridiculous and expensive forms of posturing, usually involving the deployment of military aircraft over long distances.

In the early 1980s, the Canadian government issued a land use permit to Dome Petroleum, a Canadian company, for the establishment of a scientific camp to study the impact of sea-ice and icebergs being pushed by strong currents against Hans Island's north shore. The study was intended to assist in the design of platforms and artificial islands for offshore drilling rigs. When Federal Land Use Administrator Joe Ballantyne inspected the camp in 1983, Danish military jets buzzed the island—and "scared the daylights out of the scientists."

The next year, Tom Høyem, then Danish minister for Greenland, flew to Hans Island by helicopter and planted a Danish flag. The Canadian government issued a diplomatic protest. Additional Danish flag plants—and Canadian protests—followed in 1988, 1995, 2002, 2003 and 2004.

In 2000, a team of geologists from the Geographical Society of Canada visited the island, mapped its location and took geological samples.

Despite all the activity, both sides maintained a sense of humour about the dispute. As Peter Taksoe-Jensen, the senior lawyer at the Danish Foreign Ministry, has said: "When Danish military go there, they leave a bottle of schnapps. And when [Canadian] military forces come there, they leave a bottle of Canadian Club and a sign saying, 'Welcome to Canada.'"

The dispute began to attract public attention only in 2002 as the result of an alarmist *Globe and Mail* op-ed piece entitled "The Return of the Vikings." Rob Huebert's article was prompted by the Danish ice-strengthened frigate *Vædderen* entering Kennedy Channel the previous summer and possibly landing troops on Hans Island. Just in case, the Canadian government had again issued a diplomatic protest. Huebert described the Danes as "invading hordes." The statement was farcical, since Denmark is a close NATO ally with troops fighting alongside the Canadian forces in Afghanistan. Unfortunately, the escalation of the dispute in the media played directly into the hands of Canadian and Danish politicians seeking electoral advantage.

The *Vædderen* had sailed to Hans Island just a couple of months before the Danish general election of November 2001. The 2002, 2003 and 2004 flag plants strengthened the Danish government's nationalist credentials in the lead-up to the next general election there in February 2005. Canada's response—a flag plant on July 13, 2005, followed one week later by the arrival of Defence Minister Bill Graham—occurred in the face of strong Conservative criticism about the Liberal government's failure to stand up for Canadian sovereignty in the North. Six months later, when Stephen Harper was elected prime minister, he made Arctic sovereignty the topic of his first press conference.

The role of domestic politics becomes even more apparent when one considers that the dispute over Hans Island has no implications for the location of the maritime boundary between Greenland and Ellesmere Island, or for Canadian or Danish rights elsewhere. When Canada and Denmark delimited the ocean floor between Canada and Greenland in 1973, they left a gap of only 875 metres between the end points on the north and south shores of Hans Island. Any resolution of the dispute over the island will not affect the surrounding seabed, which has already been divided by treaty. Nor will it have any consequence for the surrounding waters, since the same line has been used by both countries to define their fishing zones.

Rob Huebert was wrong to assert that an unfavourable settlement of the Hans Island dispute would, "given the important of precedence in international law," have implications for Canada's interests in the Northwest Passage and the Beaufort Sea. Hans Island is located hundreds of kilometres from the Northwest Passage and thousands of kilometres from the Beaufort Sea. The issue is also qualitatively different, since it concerns land rather than water and seabed. In the worst-case scenario, acquiescing in the Danish claim could suggest a certain lack of political resolve.

Still, even the smallest point of friction has the potential to flare into something more significant. Knowing that international politics are complex and unpredictable, countries seek to eliminate points of friction during periods of good relations, rather than risking problems later. This explains why, in September 2005, Canada and Denmark issued the following joint statement:

> We acknowledge that we hold very different views on the question of the sovereignty of Hans Island. This is a territorial dispute which has persisted since the early 1970s, when agreement was reached on the maritime boundary between Canada and Greenland. We underscore that this issue relates only to the island as such, and has no impact on that agreement.
>
> Firmly committed as we are to the peaceful resolution of disputes, including territorial disputes, we consistently support this principle here at the United Nations, and around the world. To this end, we will continue our efforts to reach a long-term solution to the Hans Island dispute. Our officials will meet again

in the near future to discuss ways to resolve the matter, and will report back to Ministers on their progress.

While we pursue these efforts, we have decided that, without prejudice to our respective legal claims, we will inform each other of activities related to Hans Island. Likewise, all contact by either side with Hans Island will be carried out in a low key and restrained manner.

Unfortunately, not all provocative actions have ceased. In February 2006, Indian and Northern Affairs Canada—in return for a $57 processing fee—granted a five-year exclusive mineral prospecting permit over Hans Island to Vancouver-based geologist John Robins. Instead of intervening to block the permit, Foreign Affairs Canada simply asked that Robins inform them before visiting the island so that they could notify Denmark.

Nevertheless, the joint statement has opened the door to a mutually beneficial compromise. In May 2008, Per Stig Møller, the Danish foreign minister, indicated that Canada and Denmark were working toward a long-term resolution of the dispute: "We both adhere to the protocol, which means we agree to disagree about who owns it. As long as we have not found out who owns it, we are working together, and we are doing that. Officials are going into papers and into history and geography and some maps."

Digging into history, geography and maps could make the difference if Canada and Denmark were willing to submit the Hans Island dispute to arbitration or litigation. But it seems unlikely that either country will wish to take the domestic political risk of losing the island before a panel of judges in Hamburg or The Hague. For the same reason, neither side is about to surrender the island during the course of negotiations, unless a compelling trade-off can be made.

Such a trade-off could be achieved in at least two ways. The first possibility is that Hans Island could be split in half by connecting the seabed delimitation line on one side to the continuation of that line on the other. Each country would have full sovereignty over 50 per cent of the island, and Canada and Europe would share a new, short and very remote land border. The second possible solution is declaring Hans Island a condominium, in the sense that Canada and Denmark would share sovereignty over all of it. There are a number of such condominiums worldwide, including Pheasant Island in the middle of the Bidasoa River between France and Spain. The two countries share sovereignty, with administrative responsibility alternating every six months between the French municipality of Hendaye and the Spanish municipality of Irún.

Inuit in Canada and Greenland should be involved in either solution, with their interests and opinions canvassed in advance. Indeed, involving the local population was suggested by Tom Høyem, the former Danish minister, in 2005:

> [L]et us together use Hans Island as a symbol of peace and good-will to show how civilized nations treat each other with respect...
> [B]oth Canadians and Danes should respect and involve the local population, not only in resolving this small dispute, but also in developing future Arctic strategy.

The governments of Greenland and Nunavut might wish to assume responsibility for managing the new border or the shared sovereignty arrangement. They might even wish to create an international park, along the lines of Waterton-Glacier International Peace Park, which straddles the border between Alberta and Montana.

Resolving the dispute over Hans Island could also pave the way toward the settlement of another Canada-Denmark dispute in the Lincoln Sea where, as we will see in Chapter 6, there is much greater potential for mutual benefit. Indeed, with just a bit of imagination and some proactive diplomacy, Hans Island could

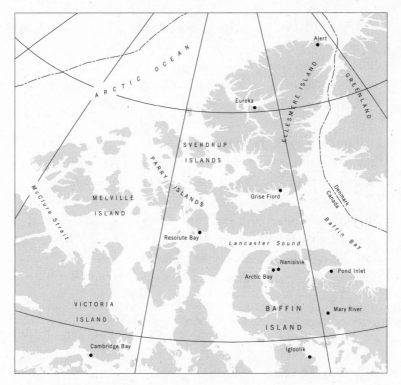

The Sverdrup Islands / SOURCE: PAUL EDMUNDS

finally be made significant—as a stepping stone to greater security and cooperation in the North.

Proactive diplomacy has protected Canada's interests before, in another potential dispute concerning the limits of its territory. Were it not for the foresight of Canadian diplomats between the First and Second World Wars, we might today be embroiled in a difficult and potentially very costly sovereignty dispute over oil and gas reserves in the Sverdrup Islands of northwestern Nunavut. Incredibly remote and historically besieged with ice, the islands were initially discovered, mapped and claimed for Norway by Otto Sverdrup, the famed Norwegian explorer, who had sailed there on his purpose-built ship the *Fram*.

Although the Norwegian government had shown little interest in Sverdrup's claim, in 1930 the Canadian government decided to close off that possibility. Negotiations were initiated, with the British government acting as an intermediary because the Statute of Westminster—which accorded Canada independence in foreign policy—would not be adopted until the following year. An offer was made to purchase Sverdrup's maps and papers concerning his voyage, thus assisting him in his retirement, in return for Norway formally recognizing Canadian sovereignty. A lump sum payment of $67,000 was agreed upon, after the Canadian government had decided that annual payments might cost too much if the seventy-six-year-old explorer lived an unusually long life. This was a bad call, since Sverdrup died just two weeks after the settlement was announced. The settlement itself took the form of an "exchange of notes," a form of international treaty comprising a series of official letters expressing an agreement between nation-states.

In a letter written on August 8, 1930, the Norwegian chargé d'affaires in London asked the British foreign secretary to "inform His Majesty's Government in Canada that the Norwegian Government, who do not as far as they are concerned claim sovereignty over the Sverdrup Islands, formally recognise the sovereignty of His Britannic Majesty over these islands." The Canadian diplomats had achieved their goal quickly and at relatively little cost, but the Norwegian chargé d'affaires had stumbled badly. Almost immediately, he wrote a second letter:

> With reference to my note of to-day in regard to my Government's recognition of the sovereignty of His Britannic Majesty over the Sverdrup Islands, I have the honour, under instructions from my Government, to inform you that the said note has been despatched on the assumption on the part of the Norwegian Government that His Britannic Majesty's Government

in Canada will declare themselves willing not to interpose any obstacles to Norwegian fishing, hunting or industrial and trading activities in the areas which the recognition comprises.

Canadian sovereignty having already been recognized, however, there was nothing left to negotiate. The Canadians could have dismissed the second letter out of hand, but instead they offered a reason for denying the request. On November 5, 1930, the British chargé d'affaires in Oslo wrote to the Norwegian Minister for Foreign Affairs:

[I]t is the established policy of the Government of Canada, as set forth in an Order in Council of July 19, 1926, and subsequent Orders, to protect the Arctic areas as hunting and trapping preserves for the sole use of the aboriginal population of the Northwest Territories, in order to avert the danger of want and starvation through the exploitation of the wild life by white hunters and traders. Except with the permission of the Commissioner of the Northwest Territories, no person other than native Indians or Eskimos is allowed to hunt, trap, trade, or traffic for any purpose whatsoever in a large area of the mainland and in the whole Arctic island area, with the exception of the southern portion of Baffin Island. It is further provided that no person may hunt or kill or traffic in the skins of the musk-ox, buffalo, wapiti, or elk. These prohibitions apply to all persons, including Canadian nationals.

Significantly, non-aboriginals were prohibited not just from hunting and trapping in the High Arctic but from *all* commercial activities there.

The letter from the British chargé d'affaires concluded with a conciliatory but meaningless offer:

Should, however, the regulations be altered at any time in the future, His Majesty's Government in Canada would treat with the most friendly consideration any application by Norwegians to share in any fishing, hunting, industrial, or trading activities in the areas which the recognition comprises.

The phrase "friendly consideration" did not create a legal right of Norwegian access to the resources of the Sverdrup Islands. However, to this day Norwegian companies are free to participate in the Canadian oil and gas industry according to the normal rules set out in the Investment Canada Act.

Canadians should be grateful for the foresight displayed in 1930 by our relatively young foreign service, because the Sverdrup Islands contain at least $1 trillion of oil and gas deposits. We know this because extensive exploration work was carried out more than a quarter of a century ago. Seismic surveys were conducted on Amund Ringnes Island and Axel Heiberg Island in the early 1970s. In the early 1980s, Panarctic Oils operated a large base camp at Rea Point on southeast Melville Island, including an airstrip built for Boeing 727 jets. A number of 5,000-metre-deep wells were drilled on Melville Island. Offshore of Lougheed Island, Panarctic laid 3,000 km of seismic grid lines and built and operated a huge drilling platform on the sea-ice. In September 1985, a shipment of oil was taken from the Bent Horn well on Cameron Island by the ice-strengthened MV *Arctic*, transferred to MV *Imperial Bedford* near Resolute Bay, and then delivered to Montreal.

Joe Ballantyne, who served as the federal land use administrator for the Arctic islands, explains that the oil companies had even greater ambitions for the field:

During the [19]70s, there was a proposal put forward called the Polar Gas Project. It entailed building a pipeline to connect the gas fields around Melville Island. A liquefied natural gas (LNG) plant was to be built on one of the Islands (possibly Melville Island) where ships would load the LNG for shipment south.

To get around the problem of ice, the plan called for submarine tankers. Quite a scheme, and a hefty price tag, too. Natural gas prices now (or soon) might justify a resurrected Polar Gas Project. With less Arctic ice, reinforced hulls on conventional tankers would likely be sufficient to move the LNG. This would be a much cheaper and more feasible alternative than using purpose-built submarine tankers.

Whether it makes environmental sense to exploit the hydrocarbons of the Sverdrup Islands is another question, though natural gas at least burns cleaner than do oil and coal.

The Sverdrup Islands are frequently referred to as the Queen Elizabeth Islands, since the Canadian government decided in 1953 to rename the Parry Archipelago (which included all of the islands north of the Northwest Passage) in honour of the new monarch. But even with their original Norwegian name, the Sverdrup Islands and their natural resources are undoubtedly Canadian. The only question left is which level of government within Canada should control and benefit from them. Devolving jurisdiction over the oil and gas of the Sverdrup Islands to Nunavut might enable the territory to develop economically without federal transfer payments. As I will explain in Chapter 7, it could also strengthen Canada's legal position in the Northwest Passage—and thus benefit us all.

Chapter Three

An Ice-Free Northwest Passage

"WHERE HAS ALL the ice gone?" Joe Immaroitok asked. It was October 24, 2006, and he was staring out over Foxe Basin. The basin, a shallow expanse of ocean the size of Lake Superior, had always frozen over by early October, enabling the Inuit to travel across to Baffin Island to hunt caribou. Now, the hamlet council in Igloolik was considering chartering an airplane to take the hunters across the unfrozen sea.

Shortly before speaking with Immaroitok, my colleague Suzanne Lalonde and I had sailed through Fury and Hecla Strait on the *Amundsen*. All we saw were a few chunks of thick, aquamarine multi-year ice, which had floated down from higher latitudes and were easily avoided. The previous day, we had passed through Bellot Strait—the first ship ever to do so in October. We were 600 km north of the Arctic Circle, but there was absolutely no ice.

The two straits that we passed through so easily are part of the Northwest Passage, the so-called Arctic Grail. From Martin Frobisher in 1576 to John Franklin in 1845, generations of European explorers had searched for a navigable route around North America to Asia. Many of them, including Franklin and his men,

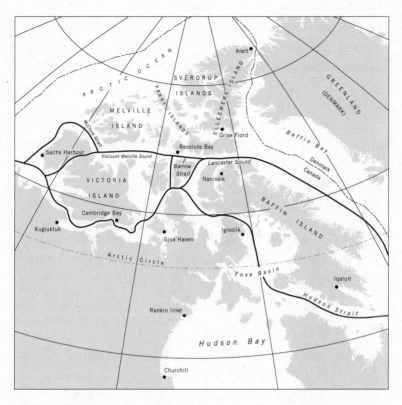

The Northwest Passage / SOURCE: PAUL EDMUNDS

died in the attempt. Their greatest challenge was sea-ice, which has almost always filled the straits, even in summer. William Parry spent the summers of 1822 and 1823 waiting for the ice to clear from Fury and Hecla Strait. But though the strait is named after his ships, he never made it through. Leopold M'Clintock, dispatched by Lady Franklin to search for her husband on King William Island, tried six times to penetrate Bellot Strait during the summer of 1858 before continuing his journey by dogsled. It took Roald Amundsen three years—including two winters lodged in the ice at Gjoa Haven—to complete the first full transit of the Northwest Passage in 1906.

The Northwest Passage is a web of several possible routes through Canada's High Arctic, a vast archipelago made up of about nineteen thousand islands and countless rocks and reefs. The widest and deepest route runs from Lancaster Sound through Barrow Strait into Viscount Melville Sound and onward through McClure Strait to the Beaufort Sea. An alternative route diverts southwest from Viscount Melville Sound through the relatively narrow but deep Prince of Wales Strait. Historically, severe ice conditions in McClure Strait and Viscount Melville Sound have forced explorers, adventurers and Coast Guard icebreakers to take a combination of more southerly routes, all of which exit into the Beaufort Sea through Coronation Gulf and Amundsen Gulf, to the south of Victoria and Banks islands. But history is little guide for what is now happening in the North.

THE BIG MELT

A strong sense of apprehension permeated the bridge of the *Amundsen* as we sailed through Bellot Strait and the forty Arctic scientists on board realized the full implications of the missing ice. It is one thing to learn from temperature gauges and remote sensing satellites that climate change is accelerating beyond all scientific expectations and another thing to see the change unfold before your eyes.

In 2004, the Arctic Climate Impact Assessment reported that the average extent of sea-ice cover in summer had declined by 15 to 20 per cent over the previous thirty years. The remaining ice was 10 to 15 per cent thinner overall and 40 per cent thinner in the middle of the Arctic Ocean. These trends were expected to accelerate, so that by the end of the twenty-first century, there might be no sea-ice at all in the summer.

Three years later, the European Space Agency released satellite images showing that the ice-covered area in the Arctic had dropped to around 3 million km^2, roughly 1 million km^2 less than the previous minimums of 2005 and 2006. The 2007 ice loss was approximately ten times greater than the average annual reduction over the previous decade. The satellite images also showed that the Northwest Passage was fully navigable, including the deep water route through McClure Strait.

In April 2009, the U.S. National Snow and Ice Data Center reported that, despite an unusually cold winter, the maximum extent of the winter sea-ice cover for 2008–09 was the fifth-lowest on record. It noted that "the six lowest maximum events since satellite monitoring began in 1979 have all occurred in the past six years." The ice was also becoming much thinner, on average, and therefore more susceptible to melting the following summer.

As early as December 2007, Wieslaw Maslowski of the U.S. Naval Postgraduate School was warning that a seasonally ice-free Arctic Ocean was possible by 2013. His prediction was obtained by adding the factor of heat absorbed by open ocean water into models based on data from 1979–2004. The dark water revealed by melting ice not only absorbs huge amounts of solar energy; it retains that energy, delaying the formation of the next winter's ice.

Despite this encroaching reality, some Canadian government scientists believe that ice conditions in the Northwest Passage will actually become worse for shipping. In 2008, Natural Resources Canada predicted:

> The longer thaw season of a warmer climate will promote a longer period of weakness in the pack, resulting in more rapid drift of Arctic Ocean multi-year ice through the Arctic Archipelago and into the Northwest Passage. This will tend to maintain, or even increase, the hazard to shipping in the Northwest Passage as long as there is a supply of ice from the Arctic Ocean.

But the fact of the matter is that, as soon as the ice melts out completely in late summer, the Northwest Passage will become navigable twelve months a year, since a complete melt will spell the end of the multi-year ice that poses the principal hazard to shipping. From that point onward, the Northwest Passage and the Arctic Ocean will resemble the Gulf of St. Lawrence or the Baltic Sea, where ice-strengthened ships and icebreaker-escorted convoys can safely operate in winter. Since this could happen as early as 2013, we should be preparing urgently for that possibility.

There is no doubt that ships will come. As noted, the Northwest Passage offers a route between East Asia and the Atlantic Seaboard that is 7,000 km shorter than the current one through the Panama Canal, saving time, fuel and transit fees. In August 2008, a Danish cable-laying ship, the MV *Peter Faber*, needed to move from a project near Taiwan to another project between Newfoundland and Greenland. The captain chose the Northwest Passage, sailing through without incident or fanfare.

The deepwater route of the Northwest Passage could also accommodate super-tankers and container ships that are too large for the Panama Canal. More and more ships are being built that exceed the "Panamax" dimensions of 294 metres by 32 metres with a maximum draft of 12 metres (giving rise to a displacement of around 65,000 tons). U.S. Navy aircraft carriers are also too big for the Panama Canal and may be attracted to an ice-free Northwest Passage.

In the near term, uncertainties about the weather, ice movements and availability of search-and-rescue will—along with higher insurance premiums—dissuade reputable international shipping companies from sending ships through Canada's Arctic Archipelago. But less solvent and less reputable companies might well take the risk, raising the prospect that some of the least safe vessels on the oceans might actually be the first to use the waterway.

Franklyn Griffiths argues that ships are much more likely to go straight "over the top," across the Arctic Ocean to the north of

Canadian territory. He is correct with respect to voyages between Asia and Europe, or between the west coast of North America and Europe. But going around Greenland adds more than 2,000 km to voyages to or from the east coast of North America, as can be discerned using a globe and a piece of string. The relatively calm waters within the archipelago will also be attractive: in 1999, a massive Russian dry dock was towed to the Bahamas through the Northwest Passage in order to reduce the risk of exposure to ocean storms. Cruise ships are already frequent visitors. Each summer now, as mentioned, more than 150 cruise ships visit the glaciers of western Greenland, while dozens explore Baffin Island's ice-capped fjords. A few ice-strengthened cruise ships also sail the Passage, with some history-conscious tourists willing to pay a premium for succeeding where so many explorers failed.

More shipping is also being generated by the increased commercial activity in Canada's Arctic. In 2007, mining companies spent $330 million in Nunavut in pursuit of gold, diamonds, uranium and other minerals. On northern Baffin Island, the Mary River iron ore mine is under development and already has hundreds of employees. With 365 million tonnes of proven and probable reserves, the mine is projected to produce 18 million tonnes per year for the next quarter of a century. The high-quality ore will be shipped directly to Europe on a fleet of 300-metre-long ice-strengthened ships purpose-built in Finland and capable of operating in Foxe Basin, Nunavut, throughout the year.

In the mineral-rich Kitikmeot region of western Nunavut, six mining companies—including giants Rio Tinto and De Beers—have joined together in support of the Bathurst Inlet Port and Road Project. The proposed port would be able to accommodate ships as large as 25,000 tons. Linked to a 211-kilometre all-weather road, it would enable the companies to bring heavy equipment in to their mines and ship the extracted ore out to market. The port would also increase traffic in the Northwest Passage, since Bathurst Inlet is on Coronation Gulf, part of the southern route of the waterway.

In September 2008, the MV *Camilla Desgagnés*, an ice-strengthened cargo ship, made a scheduled resupply run from Montreal to four communities in western Nunavut. The crew reported seeing no ice in the Northwest Passage. Desgagnés Transarctik, the company that owns the ship, has a similar voyage planned for 2009, as does its main competitor, Nunavut Eastern Arctic Shipping.

Increased shipping can also be expected to result from easier access to Arctic hydrocarbons, as climate change melts the sea-ice and renders the long-delayed Mackenzie Valley Pipeline passé. Companies are already looking to the Northwest Passage as a route for shipping oil and liquefied natural gas from northern Alaska and the Beaufort Sea to refineries and markets in eastern North America; indeed, Royal Dutch Shell has commissioned a study of the waterway. If and when the $1 trillion in proven oil and gas reserves in the Sverdrup Islands of northern Nunavut is exploited, that gas and oil too will likely be shipped east through Barrow Strait and Lancaster Sound.

THE LEGAL DISPUTE

The legal dispute over the Northwest Passage does not concern Canada's title to the waterway. Rather, the United States has long considered that the Passage, which cuts between thousands of indisputably Canadian islands, fulfills the legal criteria for an international strait by connecting two expanses of high seas (the Atlantic and Arctic oceans) and being used for international navigation. From this perspective, Canada owns the waterway, but foreign vessels have a right of "transit passage," much like walkers on a footpath through British farmland.

In contrast, Canada regards the Northwest Passage as "internal waters" having the same legal status as the Ottawa River or Lake Winnipeg. Accordingly, foreign vessels must have Canada's permission and are subject to the full force of Canadian domestic law. But while that's clear enough, Canada has changed its legal position several times in the past century—opening it up to charges of inconsistency and, perhaps, weakening the claim.

For decades, the nearly impenetrable ice meant that the issue of ownership and control rarely arose. At most, a claim to the Northwest Passage was implicit in an assertion made in 1907 by Canadian Senator Pascal Poirier that Canada owned everything within a pie-shaped sector extending from the continental coastline to the geographic North Pole. That perception of Canada's Arctic sovereignty was shared by Canadian explorer Captain J.E. Bernier, who in 1909 affixed a plaque on Melville Island that reads:

This Memorial is erected today to commemorate the taking possession for the DOMINION OF CANADA of the whole ARCTIC ARCHIPELAGO lying to the north of America from longitude 60°w. to 141°w. up to latitude 90°N.

Lester Pearson, while Canadian ambassador to the United States in 1946, made the claim over water explicit by declaring that the "sector theory" (as it was now called) justified Canada's claims "not only to the land within the sector, but to the frozen sea as well."

Yet the applicability of the sector theory to Arctic waters has never been accepted internationally. When Norway recognized Canada's sovereignty over the Sverdrup Islands in 1930, it specified that the move was "in no way based on any sanction whatever of what is named 'the sector principle.'" When the Soviet Union used the sector theory to define its Arctic territory in 1926, it chose not to apply the theory to the ice or the waters beyond the then three-mile limit of the territorial sea. The same is true in the Antarctic, where a number of countries have claimed sectors of the continent but not the outlying waters or seabed.

Faced with international opposition to its sector-based claim, the Canadian government chose neither to advance nor to explicitly abandon the argument. That is, until August 2006, when Stephen Harper surrendered the sector theory in a speech in Iqaluit:

> I am here today to make it absolutely clear there is no question about Canada's Arctic border. It extends from the northern tip of Labrador all the way up the East coast of Ellesmere Island to Alert. Then it traces the western perimeter of the Queen Elizabeth Islands down to the Beaufort Sea. From there it hugs the coasts of the Northwest Territories and Yukon to the Canada-U.S. border at Alaska. All along the border, our jurisdiction extends outward two hundred miles into the surrounding sea, just as it does along our Atlantic and Pacific coastlines. No more. And no less.

As defined by the prime minister, the limits of Canada's jurisdiction along the northwest flank of the Arctic Archipelago fall hundreds of kilometres short of the 141st meridian. But while the sector theory is dead, Canadian diplomats have spent decades developing other arguments.

The Arctic Waters Pollution Prevention Act

In 1969, Exxon sent an ice-strengthened super-tanker—the ss *Manhattan*—through the Northwest Passage. At 115,000 tons and 43,000 horsepower, it was, at the time, the largest merchant ship ever to fly the American flag. The voyage was intended to test the feasibility of the Northwest Passage as a route for shipping oil from Alaska to the Atlantic Seaboard. The U.S. government sent the Coastguard icebreaker *Northwind* to accompany the super-tanker and made a point of not seeking Canada's permission.

Concerned by the precedent the voyage might create, the Trudeau government decided the best response was a friendly offence. Although permission had not been requested, Ottawa granted it anyway, and then sent a Canadian icebreaker—the *John A. Macdonald*—to provide assistance if necessary.

The U.S. government was not, in fact, being particularly provocative, for it was not anticipated that the *Manhattan* would enter Canadian waters. Canada, along with many other countries, was still claiming only a 3-mile territorial sea in 1969, and this (in the absence of an explicit sector-based claim) left a high-seas corridor through the middle of the archipelago. The *Manhattan* planned to remain within that corridor throughout the voyage, entering through Lancaster Sound and exiting through McClure Strait. Washington even informed Ottawa that it "had no intention of staking a claim to the Northwest Passage."

However, the *Manhattan* became trapped in the heavy ice of McClure Strait on at least ten occasions, escaping only with the repeated assistance of the Canadian icebreaker. With its original plan stymied, the super-tanker headed southwest through Prince of Wales Strait, where, as Professor Donat Pharand of the University of Ottawa explained, "It had to go through the territorial waters of Canada because of the presence of the small Princess Royal Islands." Given Canada's unsolicited permission and the very heavy reliance on the Canadian Coast Guard, it is debatable whether this development created that significant a precedent.

The voyage of the *Manhattan* did send a clear signal to the Canadian government. Foreign ships would use the Northwest Passage from time to time, and Canada was poorly positioned to regulate them. A small group of international lawyers went to work, including Ivan Head (Trudeau's senior foreign policy adviser), Alan Beesley (who later chaired the drafting committee at the UN

Conference on the Law of the Sea) and a young Allan Gotlieb (who later became Canada's long-serving ambassador in Washington). The group quickly realized that Canada was not ready to confront the United States in a direct battle of legal claims and instead crafted a more roundabout but ultimately successful approach that focussed on environmental protection.

The Arctic marine ecosystem is one of the most fragile on earth, with incredibly specialized species relying on a precarious ice-water interface that is kept in balance by only fractions of a degree of temperature. The ecosystem is especially susceptible to oil spills, which as noted take decades to dissipate and degrade in cold northern waters.

The threat posed by oil spills was impressed on people's minds by the late 1960s. In 1962, the publication of Rachel Carson's *Silent Spring* had provided the impetus for the environmental movement. In 1967, the world's first major oil spill occurred when the super-tanker *Torrey Canyon* went onto the rocks off Cornwall, England. In January 1969, the blowout of an offshore rig near Santa Barbara, California, covered the area's beaches with more than eighty thousand barrels of crude oil.

Seizing the moment, the Canadian government adopted the 1970 Arctic Waters Pollution Prevention Act (AWPPA), which imposed strict safety and environmental requirements on all shipping within 100 nautical miles of Canada's Arctic coast. The Act was, at the time, contrary to international law, which did not recognize coastal state rights in the waters beyond 12 nautical miles from shore. Indeed, the Canadian government effectively admitted that the Act was inconsistent with international law when, shortly before adopting the statute, it modified its pre-existing, general acceptance of the jurisdiction of the International Court of Justice in order to block the matter from being litigated there.

The United States responded with a diplomatic protest that focussed on the precedent the Act could create: "If Canada had the right to claim and exercise exclusive pollution and resources juris-diction on the high seas, other countries could assert the right to exercise jurisdiction for other purposes, some reasonable and some not, but equally invalid according to international law." Washington suggested that Ottawa voluntarily submit the issue to the Interna-tional Court of Justice, but Ottawa did not do so. Other countries also complained about the Arctic Waters Pollution Prevention Act, as the legal adviser to the Department of External Affairs acknowl-edged when questioned by a Parliamentary committee eight years later. As he explained, a "drawer full of protests" had been received.

The dispute over the Arctic Waters Pollution Prevention Act receded after the adoption of the 1982 UN Convention on the Law of the Sea. Canadian diplomats played key roles in the negotiation of UNCLOS. Their influence is manifest in Article 234, the so-called Arctic exception, which allows coastal states to enact laws against maritime pollution out to 200 nautical miles when almost year-round ice creates exceptional navigational hazards.

Article 234 sparked the development of a parallel rule of cus-tomary international law that binds all countries, including those, like the United States, that still have not ratified UNCLOS. As early as 1985—nine years before the Convention received the sixty rati-fications necessary to come into force, and a full eighteen years before Canada itself ratified—the Canadian government decided that it was safe to once again accept the jurisdiction of the Inter-national Court of Justice unconditionally.

The United States has accepted the Arctic Waters Pollution Prevention Act, insofar as it recommends that U.S.-flagged mer-chant vessels follow the statute's provisions. However, it is unclear whether this recommendation constitutes an acceptance of Cana-da's *legal* position. Professor Bernard Oxman of the University of Miami, who represented the United States in the negotiation of Article 234, maintains that the provision does not apply in inter-national straits, since that issue was never expressly dealt with by negotiators. Professor Don McRae of the University of Ottawa responds that the negotiators, by failing to deal expressly with the application of Article 234 to international straits, were in fact indicating that they did not consider the Northwest Passage to be an international strait.

A more convincing argument is that the uncertainty surrounding the scope of Article 234, when combined with the environmental imperative behind the rule, creates a presumption that ice-covered waterways such as the Northwest Passage are not international straits. In short, an international strait in ice-covered waters that was *not* subject to strict environmental regulation by the coastal state would undermine the purpose of both Article 234 and any parallel customary rule.

Still, none of these arguments are convincing enough to guarantee acceptance by an international court. And if Article 234 was found not to apply in the Northwest Passage, efforts to protect the maritime environment in the Arctic waterway would be seriously, perhaps irreparably compromised. All of which left a question for Canadian diplomats to address in the years and decades following 1970: what is Canada's position concerning the *legal status* of the waterway, and how might it be strengthened?

Historic Internal Waters

At the same time that it adopted the Arctic Waters Pollution Prevention Act, Canada began arguing that the straits and channels between the Arctic islands were "historic internal waters." Under international law, a country making such a claim must demonstrate that it has exercised exclusive authority over the waters in question for a considerable length of time and that other countries, especially those directly affected by the claim, have consistently acquiesced in that.

Hudson Bay is a good example. Canada has claimed the 1.2 million km² expanse of water as a "historic bay" since 1906. The United States initially filed a protest, but for more than a century no country has publicly opposed the claim. Nor would it be in the U.S. national interest to do so, since shipping traffic through Hudson Bay does not lead anywhere except the port of Churchill, Manitoba. Moreover, James Bay—at the southern end of Hudson Bay—reaches to within 1,500 km of Chicago, Detroit and New York City, putting those cities within easy reach of ship-launched cruise missiles. Thanks to Hudson Bay's status as historic internal waters, Canada, in concert with NATO and NORAD, can legitimately deny access to warships of non-allies.

Canada's historic claim to the Northwest Passage relies partly on the three centuries of British exploration that began with Frobisher in 1576 and ended with the dozens of rescue expeditions sent after the Franklin expedition in the 1850s. Together, these explorers mapped most of the Arctic Archipelago, with Robert McClure discovering the existence of a full route through the Northwest Passage in 1853 by travelling west to east by dogsled. The official hand-off came when the British government transferred title over the archipelago, excluding Greenland, to Canada in 1880.

The Canadian government sought to consolidate its title in the early twentieth century by adopting legislation on whaling, sending out annual RCMP patrols and, in 1926, designating most of the archipelago as an "Arctic Islands Preserve" in order to protect wildlife and the Inuit who lived there. These actions were particularly significant because they concerned the waters between the islands and not just the land. J.E. Bernier's voyages were especially important. The Quebecois captain of the *Arctic* served in the employment of the Canadian government from 1904 to 1911, overwintering three times in the North and claiming the entire archipelago—land, water and ice—on behalf of Canada.

Donat Pharand has argued that there is a fatal flaw in Canada's historic waters argument, namely that none of this early activity was coupled with an explicit claim to the straits and channels between the islands and that later expressions of a claim have always been opposed by the United States. The fact is, very few people were thinking about the legal status of the waterway then. To the degree anyone was, they were working for the Canadian government: conducting sovereignty patrols on water and sea-ice, legislating on whaling, and protecting marine mammals and fish on behalf of a maritime people.

Indeed, the strongest element in Canada's claim is the historical occupation by the Inuit, who have hunted, fished, travelled and lived on the Northwest Passage for millennia. Alice Ayalik, who lives in Kugluktuk, is a powerful manifestation of this dimension of Canada's legal position. The seventy-two-year-old artisan spent most of the first thirteen years of her life on the frozen surface of Coronation Gulf, where her family lived in igloos, fished through the ice, and hunted seals. All along the Northwest Passage, there are hundreds of Inuit elders who, in their youth, called the frozen waterway home.

Prior to the negotiations on the Nunavut Land Claims Agreement, Inuit elders from across the Arctic were interviewed about traditional hunting and travelling patterns. The resulting maps confirmed that the waters south of Ellesmere Island and the Sverdrup Islands—including Lancaster Sound and Barrow Strait—were virtual highways for the Inuit and their dog teams. In Qikiqtarjuaq, an Inuit elder told me that he had once travelled along the east coast of Baffin Island all the way to Pond Inlet, a distance of 1,000 km, without stopping to sleep along the way.

More recently, Lynn Peplinski of the Inuit Heritage Trust has been interviewing elders about Inuktitut place names along the Northwest Passage. The literally thousands of names confirm the centrality of the frozen waterway to the Inuit's language, culture, history and identity. And the Inuit are, of course, Canadian citizens.

Their longstanding use and occupancy is the most compelling component in Canada's historic internal waters argument. What stronger claim could anyone make to the Northwest Passage than by living on it for thousands of years?

Voyage of the Polar Sea

In May 1985, Washington informed Ottawa that the Coastguard icebreaker *Polar Sea* would sail through the Northwest Passage that August, en route from the U.S. airbase at Thule, Greenland, to its home port of Seattle. The U.S. government was clear about its legal position, stating that the voyage would be "an exercise of navigational rights and freedoms not requiring prior notification." It suggested that the two countries "agree to disagree on the legal issues and concentrate on practical matters."

Ottawa responded that the Northwest Passage constituted Canadian internal waters. However, the government also indicated that it was "committed to facilitating navigation" through the waterway and was "prepared to work toward this objective." Canadian policy then, as now, was to permit Northwest Passage voyages by ships that meet the equipment and design standards of the Arctic Waters Pollution Prevention Act. According to Rob Huebert, by the end of June 1985 the two governments felt they had worked out an acceptable agree-to-disagree arrangement.

But when news of the voyage broke, it "caused a rush of public anxiety in Canada," to quote a joint House of Commons and Senate Committee that reviewed the situation the following year. Franklyn Griffiths led the charge, publishing an op-ed piece in the *Globe and Mail* entitled "Arctic authority at stake." Under pressure domestically, the Canadian government sent a diplomatic note to Washington. The note began with an expression of satisfaction "that the *Polar Sea* substantially complies with the required standards for navigation in the waters of the Arctic archipelago and that in all other respects reasonable precautions have been taken to reduce the danger of pollution arising from this voyage." And then, just as had been done with the ss *Manhattan*, the government expressly provided the permission the United States had refused to seek.

Canadian nationalists were not satisfied. Mel Hurtig, the founding president of the Council of Canadians, went so far as to charter a plane so that he could drop a Canadian flag on the deck of the *Polar Sea*. Griffiths called the Canadian government's reaction "pathetic" and, in words strikingly similar to those recently used by Stephen Harper, said: "We've got to get up there. We've got to put up or shut up about our Arctic sovereignty. To put it simply, use it or lose it for these waters."

The U.S. government seems to have neither expected nor intended the controversy. The *Globe and Mail* quoted an unidentified "senior official" in Washington as saying there was "surprise and disappointment" at the State Department, since the department had "tried to work it out so that nobody's legal rights were undercut." It was "absolutely wrong" to characterize the trip as a confrontational challenge to Canadian sovereignty, the official said.

Straight Baselines

Like the ss *Manhattan* before it, the *Polar Sea* prompted a change in the Canadian legal position. Just one month after the voyage, Foreign Minister Joe Clark announced that "straight baselines" would be used to "define the outer limit of Canada's historic internal waters." Straight baselines—lines drawn on a map between outer headlands or fringing islands—had become an accepted means for determining the extent of coastal state control along fragmented coastlines as the result of a 1951 decision by the International Court of Justice in a dispute between Britain and Norway over fishing rights. In the Arctic, straight baselines had already been employed by Denmark, Iceland and Russia.

In his speech, Clark also made reference to the unique ice-covered nature of the waters and, most importantly, to the contribution of the Inuit to Canada's legal claim:

> Canada's sovereignty in the Arctic is indivisible. It embraces land, sea and ice. It extends without interruption to the seaward facing coasts of the Arctic islands. These Islands are joined and not divided by the waters between them. They are bridged for most of the year by ice. From time immemorial Canada's Inuit people have used and occupied the ice as they have used and occupied the land.

Clark's lawyers would have drawn his attention to a 1975 judgement of the International Court of Justice in a case concerning Western Sahara, which held that nomadic peoples can acquire and transfer sovereign rights, at least over land. For the same reason, the federal government, when negotiating the Nunavut Land Claims Agreement a few years later, willingly accepted a paragraph advanced by the Inuit negotiators that affirms "Canada's sovereignty over the waters of the Arctic archipelago is supported by Inuit use and occupancy."

The United States and at least ten other countries protested the baselines, with the U.S. sending a diplomatic note stating that "there is no basis in international law to support the Canadian claim. The United States cannot accept the Canadian claim because to do so would constitute acceptance of full Canadian control of the Northwest Passage and would terminate U.S. navigation rights through the Passage under international law."

The European Community suggested that the baselines were inconsistent with international law because they were excessively long and diverted too much from the general direction of the mainland coast. Some of the lines are indeed unusually long, especially those across Lancaster Sound (51 miles), Amundsen Gulf

(92 miles) and McClure Strait (99 miles). However, in the 1951 *Anglo-Norwegian Fisheries Case*, the International Court of Justice held that "the survival of traditional rights reserved to the inhabitants of the Kingdom [of Norway] over fishing grounds...founded on the vital needs of the population and attested by very ancient and peaceful usage, may legitimately be taken into account in drawing a line." The same logic would seem to encompass the Inuit use and occupancy of the sea-ice of the Northwest Passage since "time immemorial," as referenced in Clark's speech.

It is also true that, on a map with a standard Mercator projection, the archipelago appears to jut out from the mainland. But this concern is easily addressed by consulting any map centred on the North Pole. From a circumpolar perspective, Canada's Arctic Archipelago is part and parcel of the North American coastline, rather than an appendage to it.

Used for International Navigation?

An existing international strait cannot be closed off by drawing new straight baselines. As a result, even if Canada's baselines are consistent with international law, and even if they were to be generally accepted by other countries, one crucial question remains: was the Northwest Passage an international strait prior to 1985?

Most of the international law on this point is found in the 1949 judgement of the International Court of Justice in the *Corfu Channel Case*, which identifies the decisive criteria for an international strait as "its geographical situation as connecting two parts of the high seas and the fact of its being used for international navigation." Since the Northwest Passage clearly connects two parts of the high seas, namely the Atlantic and Arctic oceans, attention has focussed on the words "being used for international navigation."

Most international lawyers interpret these words as requiring *actual* use. Donat Pharand has written that "before a strait may be considered international, proof must be adduced that it has *a history as a useful route for international maritime traffic.*" Harvard international law professor Richard Baxter agreed: "International waterways must be considered to be those rivers, canals, and straits which are used to a substantial extent by the commercial shipping or warships belonging to states other than the riparian nation or nations."

A dissenting view, to the effect that *potential* use is sufficient, has been expressed by commentators from within the U.S. military. In 1987, Richard Grunawalt of the U.S. Naval War College wrote: "Some nations take the view that an actual and substantial use over an appreciable period of time is the test. Others, including the United States, place less emphasis on historical use and look instead to the susceptibility of the strait to international navigation. The latter view has the greater merit." The last sentence is, of course, an opinion rather than an argument. Twenty years later, J.C. Kraska of the U.S. Navy stated: "The test is geographic, not functional—if the water connects one part of the high seas or EEZ [i.e., 200-nautical-mile Exclusive Economic Zone] to another part of the high seas or EEZ, it is a strait...there is no authority for the idea that a strait is only a strait if it meets a certain minimum threshold of shipping traffic."

There is, in fact, plenty of authority for that view, and the only serious debate concerns the volume of traffic necessary to create an international strait. The evidence in the *Corfu Channel Case* showed that the channel was a very useful route for ships flagged by seven states: Greece, Italy, Romania, Yugoslavia, France, Albania and the United Kingdom. Over a twenty-one-month period, there were some 2,884 transits, and this figure included only those ships that had put into port and been visited by customs agents. It did not include the large number of vessels that had transited the strait without calling at the Port of Corfu.

In contrast, Donat Pharand was able to document only sixty-nine transits of the Northwest Passage in the century prior to and including 2005: twenty small yachts, two tankers, eighteen ice-breakers and twenty-nine passenger ships. All of the foreign vessels obtained Canada's prior authorization. The only possible exceptions are the ss *Manhattan* and the *Polar Sea*, which, as we have seen, either required extensive Canadian assistance or sailed under an informal agreement-to-disagree.

When Canada proclaimed its straight baselines in January 1986, the Northwest Passage did not fulfill the functional criterion for an international strait. Had the baselines been widely recognized, it could never have become an international strait. But instead, as noted, the baselines attracted diplomatic protests from the United States and at least ten other countries. As a result, the legal status of the Northwest Passage has not yet been settled. If foreign ships begin sailing through without Canada's permission, their action could, still, turn the Northwest Passage into an international strait.

The Arctic Cooperation Agreement

The *Polar Sea* controversy and the drawing of straight baselines did have the positive effect of bringing the United States to the negotiating table. But progress was slow until Ronald Reagan came to Canada. As then Prime Minister Brian Mulroney explained almost two decades later:

> When President Reagan visited Ottawa in 1987, I showed him the Northwest Passage on an antique globe in my office and told him bluntly, "Ron, that's ours." Later, after a working lunch at 24 Sussex, he raised it with his own officials, and...instructed them to make reference to our position in his speech to Parliament.

The Arctic Cooperation Agreement was signed just a few months later, in January 1988. The United States pledged "that all navigation by U.S. icebreakers within waters claimed by Canada to be internal will be undertaken with the consent of Canada"—subject to the important proviso that "[n]othing in this Agreement... nor any practice thereunder affects the respective positions of the Governments of the United States and of Canada on the Law of the Sea in this or other maritime areas."

The Arctic Cooperation Agreement was a formal agreement-to-disagree that codified the ad hoc approach taken to the *Polar Sea* voyage. It addressed the principal irritant to Canada-U.S. relations in the Northwest Passage by taking the issue of U.S. Coastguard icebreakers out of the legal dispute. With the multi-year ice precluding voyages by other surface vessels, the deal over icebreakers created a new status quo, which might have solved the entire problem indefinitely but for the sudden, unanticipated effects of climate change two decades later, and a precipitous move by a later prime minister.

During his first prime ministerial press conference, in January 2006, Stephen Harper took aim at U.S. Ambassador David Wilkins. The previous day, while speaking to a group of students at the University of Western Ontario, the U.S. envoy had reiterated Washington's decades-old position that the Northwest Passage was an international strait. In response, Harper told reporters, "We have significant plans for national defence and for defence of our sovereignty; including Arctic sovereignty... It is the Canadian people we get our mandate from, not the ambassador from the United States."

The prime ministerial outburst generated renewed interest among Canadian parliamentarians in the Northwest Passage, which led in turn to a request being sent to the U.S. Embassy for permission to release some old diplomatic notes on the matter to MPs. The request was granted, but it opened the door for Ambassador Wilkins. In a letter to the Department of Foreign Affairs dated October 27, 2006, he adopted the strictest possible interpretation of the 1988 Arctic Cooperation Agreement and rendered that document almost meaningless:

For the record, the United States sees no basis in international law to support Canada's drawing of straight baselines around its Arctic islands and its claim that all the waters among the Canadian Arctic islands, including the Northwest Passage, are internal waters of Canada.

The Northwest Passage is a strait used for international navigation. Therein, all ships and aircraft enjoy the right of transit passage, in accordance with international law as reflected in the 1982 Law of the Sea Convention. The enjoyment of transit passage is not subject to prior notice to, or permission from, Canada as the State bordering the strait. However, an activity that is not an exercise of the right of transit passage, such as marine scientific research, remains subject to the other applicable provisions of international law.

Canada, consistent with its right as a coastal State under international law, requires that marine scientific research may be conducted in its waters only with its consent. Accordingly, as set out in the Agreement on Arctic Cooperation of January 11, 1988, the United States agrees to seek Canada's consent when U.S. icebreakers intend to conduct marine scientific research as they transit the Northwest Passage...

The Agreement expressly provides that neither it nor any practice thereunder affects the legal views of the two Parties. Thus, the Agreement does not affect the U.S. view that our icebreakers, in the absence of marine scientific research, would not be required to seek Canadian consent before transiting the Northwest Passage.

As a result of Stephen Harper's unnecessary and all-too-personal intervention, the Arctic Cooperation Agreement means much less today than most people—including Brian Mulroney—had assumed.

Chapter Four

The Northwest Passage
in Contemporary Policy

SECURITY CHALLENGES

Soviet submarines in the Northwest Passage posed a serious security threat to both Canada and the United States during the Cold
War. The ice-covered waterway offered the subs an alternative route
between the Arctic and Atlantic oceans—no small attraction
given the amount of NATO attention paid to the Greenland-Iceland-
UK gap. If Canada and the United States had been able to agree
that the Northwest Passage was Canadian internal waters, the two
countries would have had a strong legal basis for excluding the
Soviets. But while it was a given that Canada would always allow
American vessels access, the U.S. Navy was concerned about securing maximum freedom of navigation worldwide, and it worried
that recognizing Canada's claim might create a precedent for
coastal state control over other contested waterways.

In every other respect, the two NATO allies worked closely
together to counter the Soviets. They built and operated the DEW
Line, a string of fifty-eight radar stations stretching from Alaska to

Greenland. It is also well known, though not publicly admitted, that Canada and the U.S. cooperated in the deployment of underwater surveillance devices at various choke points in the Canadian Arctic Archipelago. In the early 1980s, the Department of National Defence received a federal land use permit to install a listening device off Skull Point, near the weather station at Eureka. According to Coast Guard personnel, Canadian icebreakers were frequently used in such missions. More recently, the Department of National Defence has been working to replace and improve these surveillance systems through the Northern Watch Technology Demonstration project, which involves trials of underwater and land-based sensors at Gascoyne Inlet on the north shore of Barrow Strait, halfway through the Northwest Passage.

The submarine threat still exists today, but it pales in comparison with concerns about "rogue states" and terrorist groups using the Northwest Passage to traffic in weapons of mass destruction (WMD), equipment for enriching nuclear isotopes, and missiles. Unlikely as these risks might seem at first, it is not difficult to imagine a captain in charge of this kind of cargo choosing an ice-free, under-policed Northwest Passage over a closely scrutinized Panama Canal. For this reason, transnational criminal activity and other threats from non-state actors were central to an Arctic Capabilities Study conducted by the Canadian Directorate of Defence in 2000.

Since the September 11, 2001, attacks on the World Trade Center and the Pentagon, concerns about global terrorism and WMD have greatly increased. In 2003, the United States led the creation of the Proliferation Security Initiative. This cooperative exercise has seen more than sixty countries commit to using their existing rights under international law—within their ports and territorial seas and on ships carrying their flags—to prevent the high seas from being used as an avenue for proliferating WMD. Canada is one of the participating countries.

Drug smugglers, gunrunners and illegal immigrants could also take advantage of an ice-free Northwest Passage. It would be relatively easy to transfer passengers or cargo from an ocean-going vessel to a small plane on one of dozens of gravel airstrips scattered along the waterway for travel to another small airstrip farther south. And every summer, as noted, hundreds of undocumented foreign nationals from cruise ships go ashore at communities such as Pangnirtung, Pond Inlet, Grise Fiord and Resolute Bay that have scheduled air service but no immigration controls.

Stories of attempted illegal entries, like that of the two Turkish sailors who jumped ship at Churchill and the Romanian man who sailed a small motorboat from Greenland to Grise Fiord, abound in Canada's Arctic. In 1999, the Chinese research icebreaker MV *Xuě Lóng* arrived unannounced in Tuktoyaktuk; when some of the scientists wanted to come ashore, an immigration officer had to fly up from Yellowknife to process them. There is even a regular charter flight from Frankfurt to Whitehorse, Yukon, that requires the occasional deportation back to Germany.

Having the Northwest Passage recognized as Canadian internal waters would help to prevent the illegal entry of people and goods into North America. Within internal waters, the full force of the coastal state's immigration, customs and criminal laws apply, and foreign vessels, crews, passengers and cargo can be closely scrutinized. Cargo manifests and crew and passenger lists can be required in advance, as can visas, in the same manner as on land.

In contrast, the right of transit passage has almost absolute precedence in an international strait. Under the UN Convention on the Law of the Sea, the coastal state may adopt laws concerning "the loading or unloading of any commodity, currency or person in contravention of [its] customs, fiscal, immigration or sanitary laws and regulations." But even these laws "shall not...have the practical effect of denying, hampering or impairing the right of transit passage."

For Canada and the United States, shared security concerns necessitate a real and effective presence in the Northwest Passage. For Canada, environmental concerns contribute to the same imperative, as does the need to provide search-and-rescue, navigation assistance and icebreaking for commercial vessels. Canada must also be present to prevent unauthorized crossings by foreign vessels, since any such voyages would weaken our country's legal claim, to our detriment—and to the long-term detriment of the United States and other responsible countries, as well as reputable shipping companies.

Yet Canada is poorly equipped to police its northern waters. Despite the effects of climate change, the Coast Guard's relatively light icebreakers still cannot operate in the Northwest Passage in winter; they are redeployed to the Gulf of St. Lawrence each autumn. The Coast Guard ships are also growing old. The largest, the *Louis S. St. Laurent*, was built in 1969; the *Amundsen* is just a decade younger. In 1985, after the voyage of the *Polar Sea*, the Canadian government announced that it would build a powerful all-season icebreaker, the *Polar 8*. However, four years later it cancelled the contract, citing the need for fiscal restraint. Despite subsequent years of federal surpluses, in the ensuing two decades no new icebreakers have been built.

In November 2005, then Opposition leader Stephen Harper seized on Arctic sovereignty as an election issue. He promised three armed heavy icebreakers, a deep-water port on Baffin Island, underwater sensors and Arctic-trained paratroopers. To his credit, as prime minister he has followed up on several of these promises, while taking some unexpected steps as well.

The first unexpected step came in May 2006, when the functions of the bilateral U.S.-Canada North American Aerospace Defense Command were expanded to include surveillance over maritime approaches and "internal waterways." During the House of Commons debate on the matter, then Defence Minister Gordon O'Connor was asked whether the Northwest Passage was included within the proposed new arrangement. O'Connor initially indicated that it was not, but he rose the next weekday on a point of order to correct the assertion.

The public agreement to share maritime surveillance within the Northwest Passage reinforces a longstanding practice. Again, it is well known, though not publicly acknowledged, that U.S. acoustic devices were placed in the waterway during the Cold War with full Canadian cooperation. The fact that Canada is now developing its own acoustic capabilities reflects the age of those existing devices, rather than any falling-out between the two countries. Indeed, it is possible that the development of a purely Canadian capability was what prompted the expansion of the NORAD agreement.

The second unexpected step came in July 2007, when Harper announced that six to eight ice-strengthened "Arctic Offshore Patrol Ships" would be built for the Canadian navy. The ships became the central component of his northern strategy. Six months later, $720 million was allocated for a powerful new icebreaker for the Coast Guard. The proposed ship was even given a name, the *Diefenbaker*, in honour of a previous Progressive Conservative prime minister. In June 2009, however, the navy's project management office told potential contractors that the "letter of intent" phase for the Arctic Offshore Patrol Ships was being indefinitely delayed. The *Diefenbaker* was also put on hold, though government media relations officers insist the process of determining operational requirements is ongoing. As was the case when the *Polar 8* contract was cancelled in 1990, all eyes are focussed on the spiralling deficit. Nobody at the Treasury Board regards Arctic Offshore Patrol Ships and icebreakers as core spending priorities.

The decision to suspend the projects was made easier when officials realized they had selected the wrong vessels for the job.

When the Department of National Defence sold the idea of Arctic Offshore Patrol Ships to Cabinet, the idea was to have naval vessels that could stand up to foreign states. Russian scientists had just planted their titanium flag at the North Pole, and the media was playing up the prospects for a new Cold War. Now, with all the Arctic countries working peacefully to resolve their disputes, it has become apparent that the security threat—such as it is—comes from non-state actors such as drug smugglers and illegal immigrants. In response, the navy had, before the suspension of the project, already scaled back the planned size and speed of the vessels, as well as the calibre of the deck-mounted guns.

The Arctic Offshore Patrol Ships were also compromised, from the start, by a decision to build them as ice-strengthened rather than icebreaking vessels. The plan was to make them useful in ice-free waters on the Atlantic and Pacific coasts, but this meant that purpose-built icebreakers were still needed with the ability to go anywhere, any time, in the North. Nor was there ever any intent that the Arctic Offshore Patrol Ships would fulfill the federal government's other responsibilities in northern waters, such as breaking ice for commercial vessels, maintaining navigation devices, resupplying weather stations and supporting Arctic research.

When the government decided to build the *Diefenbaker*, it erred again. Initially, the new icebreaker was due to be operational in 2017, by which point, the latest scientific projections suggest, the Arctic will already have experienced a complete summer melt-out of sea-ice. As a result, the main obstacle to shipping—thick, hard multi-year ice—will have disappeared. From that point onward, the Northwest Passage will resemble the Gulf of St. Lawrence, where mid-sized icebreakers are sufficient. By then, the powerful *Diefenbaker* would be overkill.

The recent decision to delay both projects provides the government an opportunity to get things right. Three or four mid-sized, multi-purpose Coast Guard icebreakers should be contracted immediately, with a light machine gun mounted on each forward deck. A handful of RCMP or Canadian Forces personnel should be deployed on each vessel, or, alternatively, Coast Guard crew members trained and "double-hatted" as auxiliary RCMP officers or members of the naval reserve. Either approach would be substantially less expensive than the combined costs of the Arctic Offshore Patrol Ships and the *Diefenbaker*, and better suited to the challenges we face.

At the same time the prime minister announced the Arctic Offshore Patrol Vessels, he indicated that a deepwater port would be developed at Nanisivik, a disused lead and zinc mine on northern Baffin Island. The decision was met with dismay by political leaders in Nunavut who had lobbied hard for a similar facility at Iqaluit, on southern Baffin Island, to boost economic development and reduce the high cost of living there. In any event, the announcement did not amount to much, since the wharf—composed of three concrete bollards—was built decades ago to service the mine. For years, it has been managed by the Coast Guard, which uses it to transfer supplies and store oil-spill equipment. The only change resulting from the announcement will be a shift in authority over the site from the Coast Guard to the navy, which is years away from having ships that can reach it.

Another of the prime minister's announcements promised the creation of the Canadian Forces Arctic Training Centre. A centre of this kind makes sense, because the Canadian Forces are called upon to provide search-and-rescue and disaster relief across this frequently frigid country. But again, the facility already exists, at Resolute Bay, in the form of the modern and comfortable accommodation block constructed and maintained by the Polar Continental Shelf Project on behalf of Arctic scientists. All that has changed is that the Canadian Forces now use the building for several months each winter, when it is not required by researchers.

The prime minister also announced an expansion of the Canadian Ranger program to 5,000 personnel. The program is currently composed of 4,100 part-time reservists—many of them Inuit, Inuvialuit or First Nations—who live in 165 hamlets stretching from Baffin Island to the Alaskan frontier. The Rangers, equipped with snowmobiles and old but reliable bolt action rifles, fulfill essential search-and-rescue and surveillance functions close to where they live. They also teach regular Canadian Forces personnel how to survive and travel on the land, especially in winter, and sometimes lead them on "sovereignty ops" across the ice and tundra. However, the abilities of the Rangers are dwarfed by the expanse over which they operate, and they are neither equipped nor trained to forcibly board ocean-going vessels.

By far the most significant contribution the Harper government has made to Arctic sovereignty concerns RADARSAT-2, a remote sensing satellite. Owned by the Canadian company MacDonald, Dettwiler and Associates (MDA), RADARSAT-2 was largely funded by the Liberal government of Jean Chrétien, in return for large amounts of imagery-on-demand. The satellite has been in a polar orbit 800 km above the earth's surface since December 2007, and it produces images so fine that one can discern individual hydro-transmission cables.

Although useful for monitoring crops and forests, coordinating disaster relief operations, and supporting fisheries enforcement, RADARSAT-2 was designed specifically with the Arctic in mind. It is the perfect tool for tracking ships, mapping sea-ice, and even—rumour has it—detecting the wakes of submerged submarines. And because it uses radar rather than optical technology, the satellite works regardless of darkness or clouds, an important advantage in a part of the world subject to months of total darkness and frequent overcast conditions. RADARSAT-2's usefulness for Arctic surveillance was demonstrated within weeks of its launch, when its imagery showed a ship-track through the ice in the Beaufort Sea. An airplane was sent to investigate and, sure enough, discovered a Russian icebreaker.

In January 2008, MDA announced plans to sell its space division, including RADARSAT-2, to Alliant Techsystems of Minnesota. The proposed sale sparked a firestorm of criticism, some of which focussed on the possible consequences for Canada's ability to obtain imagery of the Northwest Passage on demand. In response, then Industry Minister Jim Prentice extended the period for considering the proposed sale under the Investment Canada Act, and then blocked the sale outright.

The Canadian Forces have moved to take advantage of RADARSAT-2 by building dedicated ground stations on the Atlantic and Pacific coasts. However, if the satellite is to be put to full use, a third ground station is needed in the North. Ideally, the new facility would be incorporated into the High Arctic Research Station announced by Indian and Northern Affairs Minister Chuck Strahl in February 2009.

Surprisingly, the Harper government has paid almost no attention to the military's most important function in the Arctic—namely, search-and-rescue. Four old, slow Twin Otter aircraft based in Yellowknife constitute the entirety of the Canadian Forces northern fleet. C-130 Hercules cargo planes based in Trenton, Ontario, are relied on for most of the serious search-and-rescues, but the planes take six hours to reach the Northwest Passage and, once there, can only drop search-and-rescue technicians (SAR-techs) rather than hoist anyone on board. The government has talked about purchasing fifteen to nineteen new fixed-wing search-and-rescue aircraft. The Department of National Defence would clearly prefer Italian-built C-27J Spartans, to the point where Industry Canada blocked the procurement in June 2009 because of concerns that the specifications were deliberately drawn to exclude competitor aircraft. When new planes are finally bought, a few of them might be deployed in Yellowknife, though there is no plan to base SAR-techs with them.

None of the Canadian Forces' Cormorant search-and-rescue helicopters are based in the Arctic, not even in summer. Federal bureaucrats consider it inefficient to locate search-and-rescue assets in the North, given the sparse population and consequently low probability of accidents. But the Arctic is a large, inhospitable place, and when accidents occur they tend to be serious. At present, Cormorant helicopters are deployed in response to emergencies from southern locations, as was the case in February 2007 when an aircraft from Canadian Forces Base Comox on Vancouver Island flew thousands of kilometres to rescue an Inuvialuit hunter trapped on an ice floe off Cape Parry, Northwest Territories.

The financial cost of these long-range missions can escalate quickly: in June 2006, the Canadian Forces deployed one Hercules aircraft from Trenton, Ontario; two Hercules aircraft from Winnipeg, Manitoba; one Aurora aircraft from Greenwood, Nova Scotia; and one Cormorant helicopter from Gander, Newfoundland—all to rescue three Inuit hunters whose boat had run out of fuel near Hall Beach, Nunavut.

Cruise ships are a particular concern, because of the often large number of elderly passengers on board. When the German-owned *Hanseatic* went aground near Cambridge Bay in 1996, all of the passengers had to be evacuated. In November 2007, the Canadian-owned MS *Explorer* sank during an Antarctic voyage after hitting a small iceberg; fortunately, the sea was calm, two other cruise ships were close by, and all the crew and passengers were saved. The MS *Explorer*, a frequent visitor to Arctic waters, could just as easily have sunk in the Northwest Passage in rough seas, with no help within hours or days.

Search-and-rescue is also needed for airplane accidents, some of which could require a large-scale deployment. In 1991, a Canadian Forces Hercules crashed 20 km from Canadian Forces Station Alert on Ellesmere Island, killing five of the eighteen passengers and crew. The thirteen survivors endured two days in a raging blizzard before a search-and-rescue team from southern Canada could reach them.

More than ninety thousand commercial flights take "trans-polar" or "high latitude" routes over Canadian territory each year. The prospect of a Boeing 777 or an Airbus A340 crash-landing in the High Arctic is terrifying, even if the reliability of such aircraft means the risk is very low. Retired colonel Pierre Leblanc says that the prospect of a commercial airline accident was the one thing that kept him awake at night during his many years commanding Canadian Forces Northern Area (since renamed Joint Task Force North). When I asked Leblanc's successor, Colonel Norm Couturier, what would happen if a large jet crash-landed on Ellesmere Island in winter, his response was emphatic: "We could not get there."

Basing two Cormorants in the Arctic during the summer months would not solve the problem, but it would help. Iqaluit, Nunavut, and Inuvik, Northwest Territories, are already equipped as forward operating locations for CF-18s. From there, the Cormorants could cover the two areas of greatest maritime activity in the Canadian Arctic—Baffin Bay and the Beaufort Sea—as well as the Northwest Passage. They could then be redeployed to the east and west coasts in time for the winter storms that create the greatest search-and-rescue needs there.

Improving search-and-rescue capacity in the Northwest Passage would also facilitate the enforcement of Canadian laws and thus the credibility of our sovereignty claim. A long-range helicopter is the perfect platform for boarding ocean-going vessels. For this reason, a handful of RCMP or Canadian Forces personnel trained and equipped for armed interdictions should probably accompany any Cormorant deployed in the North.

In the summer months, Coast Guard icebreakers provide some search-and-rescue coverage. However, the helicopters based on the ships are single-pilot Messerschmitt-Bölkow-Blohm aircraft, which were sold to the Mulroney government by the notorious Karlheinz Schreiber. Their small size (four passengers) and short range (350 km) limit their effectiveness. As a point of comparison, a Cormorant can carry up to thirty passengers and fly more than 1,000 km without refuelling. The icebreakers should be provided with more capable helicopters as a matter of priority.

EXTENDING THE ARCTIC WATERS POLLUTION PREVENTION ACT

As explained in Chapter 3, Article 234 of the 1982 UN Convention on the Law of the Sea allows coastal states to apply stringent pollution prevention laws out to 200 nautical miles from shore in waters where almost year-round ice creates exceptional navigational hazards. The geographic reach of the provision is twice that of the 100 nautical miles claimed under Canada's 1970 Arctic Waters Pollution Prevention Act.

Article 234 was a major negotiating coup for Canadian diplomats seeking to legitimize the Arctic Waters Pollution Prevention Act. This makes it difficult to understand why, for more than a quarter century, no Canadian government bothered to update the legislation to take full geographic advantage. Finally, in August 2008, Prime Minister Stephen Harper announced that the definition of "Arctic waters" in the Act would be changed, so that 200 rather than 100 nautical miles became the outer limit of Canada's pollution prevention jurisdiction in the North. A bill was passed with all-party support, and the modification became law on June 11, 2009.

MAKING NORDREG MANDATORY

Canada's maritime registration system in the Arctic is called NORDREG. Created in 1977 under the Arctic Waters Pollution Prevention Act, it applies to all ships larger than 300 tons, and registration is voluntary. In contrast, the parallel systems on the Atlantic and Pacific coasts of Canada are mandatory, and for years the Coast Guard has been pressing for NORDREG to be brought into line with those.

Despite the system's voluntary character, 98 per cent of all ships already register under NORDREG. But according to a report produced in 2009 by the Standing Senate Committee on Fisheries and Oceans, when Transport Canada and Coast Guard representatives were asked about the remaining 2 per cent of vessels that do not comply, "the officials said they knew nothing about them (e.g., what they were)."

Historically, the voluntary status of NORDREG—and the government's reluctance to change it—apparently results from concerns that making the system mandatory might provoke a negative response from the United States. Franklyn Griffiths has come to the same conclusion. However, he offers the useful observation that making NORDREG mandatory actually could address contemporary U.S. concerns about improving North American security:

> As a result [of the system being voluntary], Canada does not know as much as it should about passengers, cargo, and vessel purposes. Some foreign cruise ships have failed to register with NORDREG and, as a result, Canadian officials have not had passenger and crew lists for them—even though many of the passengers are debarking at places like Resolute Bay and boarding charter flights south. Mandatory reporting could, therefore, become part of a systematic Canadian effort to tighten security against terrorist and other threats in northernmost North America.

In August 2008, during a trip to Inuvik, Northwest Territories, Stephen Harper announced that his government would in fact be making NORDREG mandatory. In doing so, he expressly anticipated some diplomatic opposition. "It'll be interesting to see. I expect that some countries may object," Harper told reporters. "I think it ultimately is in everybody's interest to ensure there is some kind of authority in the area, some kind of environmental and commercial authority...We have no particular power play here."

After the announcement, a spokesperson for the U.S. Embassy in Ottawa told CanWest News Service, "We will be discussing the proposal with Canada. We will want to ensure that any enhanced protection of the Canadian Arctic marine environment is achieved in a manner that is consistent with the international law of the sea."

It is not clear that making NORDREG mandatory would challenge the U.S. position that the Northwest Passage is an international strait. Australia has managed to secure the support of the International Maritime Organization for a compulsory reporting scheme for ships transiting Torres Strait between Australia and Papua New Guinea. As Australian law professor Stuart Kaye has explained: "It would seem that compulsory reporting does not amount to a restriction preventing vessels from using an international strait, but rather it can be construed as a matter relating to international navigation. While not strictly the designation of sea lanes or a traffic separation scheme, the reporting procedures are certainly directed solely at safety of navigation."

Unfortunately, the U.S. Embassy's concerns seem to have slowed the Harper government down. As of August 2009, a full year after the prime minister's announcement, the necessary regulatory amendment has not yet been made.

Obviously, the Government of Canada should pursue the support of the International Maritime Organization for a mandatory version of NORDREG. It should also, consistent with a recommendation of the Standing Senate Committee on Fisheries and Oceans, consider making the registration system applicable to all foreign vessels, regardless of their size. But the government should not hesitate in making the existing NORDREG system mandatory immediately. If Canada is to convince others that it is serious about protecting the maritime environment within the Northwest Passage, it should seize upon every reasonable opportunity to do so. Such actions demonstrate belief in the validity of Canada's legal position, show a real commitment to taking the steps necessary to provide a safe and efficient shipping route, and thus promote long-term support and acquiescence on the part of other states.

PROTECTING LANCASTER SOUND

For over twenty-five years, Canada and the United Nations Educational, Scientific and Cultural Organization (UNESCO) have discussed designating Lancaster Sound as a World Heritage Site. Lancaster Sound is home to endangered bowhead whales, most of the world's narwhals and one-third of North America's belugas, as well as to walrus, polar bears, ringed, bearded and harp seals and millions of seabirds. Designating Lancaster Sound a World Heritage Site would facilitate efforts to regulate shipping routes and the frequency of shipping, so as to reduce the impact on those animals, and in the process strengthen Canada's claim that the Northwest Passage constitutes internal waters subject to Canadian regulation and control. But successive Canadian governments have never pursued the designation process to completion—again, apparently because of concerns that doing so might provoke a challenge from the United States.

The less controversial domestic step of designating Lancaster Sound as a national marine conservation area—the equivalent of a national park—has also been delayed for decades, though Inuit concerns about possible limitations on hunting rights are partly responsible for this. In 2007, the federal government allocated $5 million for a five-year study as to whether such a conservation area would be "a practical approach to sustainable management in Lancaster Sound." The answer is probably no, since without the international recognition that comes with a World Heritage Site designation, foreign ships might ignore domestic environmental protections. The creation of a national marine conservation area should be coupled with a push to secure UNESCO designation, linking the domestic to the international in a mutually supportive way.

Chapter Five

Negotiating over the Northwest Passage

THE SILENT THREAT TO CANADIAN SOVEREIGNTY

When Defence Minister Peter MacKay complained about Russian bombers flying over the Beaufort Sea in February 2009, opposition politicians accused him of seeking to draw public attention away from the economic crisis. That may be true, but the kerfuffle may have been designed to conceal something else, too. A greater threat to Canada's Arctic sovereignty was running—silent and deep—in the form of a U.S. submarine that likely traversed the Northwest Passage that same week.

The day after MacKay's press conference, the *Los Angeles Times* reported on Ice Exercise 2009, a classified mission described by the U.S. Navy as the "testing of submarine operability and war-fighting capability" in the Arctic Ocean. Two nuclear-powered attack submarines, USS *Helena* and USS *Annapolis*, were heading north to test their communications equipment in the waters around and below a research station on the sea-ice some 300 km north of Prudhoe Bay, Alaska. According to the L.A. *Times*, the *Helena* had recently left its home port of San Diego. It was unclear when the other submarine had departed for the Arctic. But we do know that the *Annapolis* is based in Groton, Connecticut—and that is the rub.

There are two obvious routes from Connecticut to northern Alaska. The first involves a long detour to the east and north around Greenland, entirely within international waters. The second route takes a 2,000-kilometre shortcut through the Northwest Passage, which, as we have seen, Canada considers "internal waters" and the United States asserts is an "international strait."

Submarine transits are of central importance to understanding the U.S. position. During the Cold War, nuclear-powered submarines stalked the depths of the Arctic Ocean, which was strategically located between North America and the Soviet Union. The U.S. Navy, focussed on maintaining maximum access for its vessels in the Arctic and elsewhere, was concerned about the legal consequences for submarine traffic if the Northwest Passage was regarded as anything other than an international strait. Under the law of the sea, submarines may pass through an international strait without surfacing or otherwise alerting the adjacent coastal state or states. In internal waters, coastal state permission is required for any voyage, whether on the surface or submerged.

Nuclear-powered submarines do not require oxygen for propulsion and are therefore not dependent on the surface of the water being free of ice. It is no secret that U.S. submarines—and probably British, French and Soviet (now Russian) vessels—have regularly used the Northwest Passage in the past and likely continue to do so. An American submariner once confessed to me that he had sailed through, and Inuit hunters still report seeing the occasional periscope. What is not clear in these cases is whether Canada's permission has been sought and granted.

Publicly, Canada has chosen to ignore the issue. This country has never possessed a submarine that could travel under the ice. In 1987, the Canadian government decided to acquire ten to twelve nuclear-powered submarines that could have done so, but pressure from Washington soon led to the abandonment of that plan. Nor has Canada made any effort to deploy surface-based anti-submarine capability in the North.

Ironically, total ignorance of the voyages would work in Canada's favour. In international law, a country must show some sense of legal entitlement or obligation before its actions can contribute to establishing a new right, and this is impossible to do without knowledge. However, it seems likely that Canada—a NATO ally of Britain, France and the United States—has known about at least some of the submarine voyages and simply kept quiet. Such a combination of knowledge and passive acquiescence could prove fatal to Canada's legal position, were evidence of it made public, since this would establish actual non-consensual usage of the Northwest Passage by international shipping.

It is just as likely that any U.S. (and probably NATO) submarine traffic takes place with Canada's expressed consent. In November 1995, then Defence Minister David Collenette was asked in the House of Commons about submarines in the Northwest Passage. He replied: "Mr. Speaker, we have a number of bilateral agreements with the United States. One of them provides for the movement of U.S. vessels in Canadian waters upon agreement of such a manoeuvre...When the U.S. requires such permission, they let us know that they intend to use our waters and we acquiesce."

When Reform MP Jay Hill sought to verify that statement, Collenette corrected himself. In a letter addressed to Hill in 1996, he wrote: "There is no formal agreement covering the passage of any nation's submarines through Canadian Arctic waters. However, as a country that operates submarines, Canada does receive information on submarine activities from our allies. This information is exchanged for operational and safety reasons with the emphasis on minimizing interference and the possibility of collisions between submerged submarines." A decade later, another Liberal defence minister referred to the arrangement as a "protocol." Bill Graham assured the *Globe and Mail* in December 2005 that the United States "would have told us" before any of their submarines transited Canadian waters.

But because Canada's submarines are diesel-powered, and so cannot operate under the ice for any significant period of time, foreign submarines need not worry about colliding with them in the Arctic. That means—from a practical perspective—that foreign governments have little interest in telling us where their subs are.

In light of the probable voyage of the *Annapolis* through the Northwest Passage—and the likelihood of other transits—it is important that Canadians be informed about the specifics of the situation. If there is a bilateral agreement on submarine voyages, it would likely be modelled on the arrangement concerning icebreakers, which specifies that voyages by U.S. Coastguard icebreakers are "without prejudice" to either country's legal claim. But again, if Canada is told about the voyages without being asked for permission, that combination of knowledge and acquiescence could fatally undermine its legal position. With the key criterion for an international strait being usage by international shipping without the consent of the coastal state, a failure to protest against the submarine transits could constitute evidence that—in the corridors of international diplomacy, where it really matters—Canada has already surrendered its claim.

Taking physical action against the submarines is neither necessary nor practical. In international law, protests are sufficient to prevent the protested action from creating a new right. It is also true that the issue of submarine voyages remains off the table, legally speaking, as long as both Canada and the United States continue to treat these activities as officially secret. But keeping secrets is becoming ever more difficult in a rapidly melting, increasingly busy Arctic. The issue of the Northwest Passage can no longer be avoided. It is time to stop the shenanigans and negotiate a comprehensive agreement on shipping in those waters—before it's too late.

U.S. INTERESTS ARE CHANGING

The United States' security interests in the Arctic have, as discussed, been changed by the end of the Cold War, 9/11, and the disappearing sea-ice. Washington is now less concerned about the presence of Russian submarines than about terrorists finding a back door to North America, or rogue states using the Northwest Passage to transport the components for WMD. And the fact is that these new threats would best be dealt with through Canadian domestic law, enforced by an enhanced Coast Guard, RCMP and Canadian Forces presence. It simply does not benefit the United States—and other responsible countries and reputable shipping companies—to have foreign vessels shielded from scrutiny and reasonable regulations by maintaining that the Northwest Passage is an international strait.

Access to the waterway is not really at issue. Canada and the United States are partners in the shared defence of North America, whether at the level of border security, NORAD or NATO. Indeed, in 2006 the NORAD agreement was expanded to encompass joint maritime surveillance, including over the Northwest Passage. As long ago as 1969, Pierre Trudeau declared that "to close off those waters and to deny passage to all foreign vessels in the name of Canadian sovereignty...would be as senseless as placing barriers across the entrances of Halifax and Vancouver harbours."

However, while American experts sometimes express sympathy for Canadian concerns about the Northwest Passage, they invariably see an insurmountable obstacle to any change in the U.S. position. The concept of the freedom of the seas and the strategic mobility it provides has long been a cornerstone of U.S. foreign policy. As a result, the concern is that recognizing Canada's claim could create a precedent for other key waterways, including by encouraging coastal states elsewhere to unilaterally impose restrictions within international straits.

That concern is misplaced for several reasons. First, the Canadian position does not seek to create an exception to the international straits regime. Rather, the position is that the Northwest Passage is not and has never been an international strait.

Second, the Northwest Passage can readily be distinguished from international straits elsewhere because of its length (1,200 km or more, depending on the route) as well as the historic presence of sea-ice. As explained in Chapter 3, the distinct character of ice-covered waters was recognized in Article 234 of the UN Convention on the Law of the Sea and, arguably, excluded from the international straits regime.

Third, as Professor Suzanne Lalonde of the Université de Montréal pointed out to me, the status of most of the other waterways the U.S. sought to maintain as international straits has now been resolved. A number of them, including the Turkish Straits (Bosporus and Dardanelles), the Strait of Malacca and Torres Strait, are recognized as international straits in bilateral and multilateral treaties. A bilateral agreement between Canada and the U.S. would not destabilize these treaty regimes. Moreover, these and other international straits also have very high volumes of maritime traffic, which is enough to guarantee, on the basis of historical usage, that the right of transit passage would remain in place—regardless of what happens in Canada's North.

In reality, the Northwest Passage dispute has possible consequences for only one other waterway: the Northern Sea Route on the Russian side of the Arctic Ocean. However, sea-ice is disappearing so quickly that any ship wanting to sail that way can already do so in late summer by proceeding over the north side of the Russian islands that delimit the channels forming the Northern Sea Route. It is also inconceivable that the United States would physically challenge Russia over the status of that waterway. Americans should ask themselves: is maintaining a legal position of no real utility along the northern coast of Russia worth the security risk, from non-state actors, that will arise along the northern coast of this continent if the Northwest Passage is treated as an international strait?

The uniqueness of the situation explains why Paul Cellucci has called for Washington to recognize Ottawa's claim. In October 2004, the U.S. ambassador said: "We are looking at everything through the terrorism prism. Our top priority is to stop the terrorists. So perhaps when this is brought to the table again, we may have to take another look." Five months later, Cellucci revealed that he had asked the State Department to re-examine the U.S. position in light of the terrorist threat. And in October 2006, the by-then former ambassador made his personal views clear: "It is in the security interests of the United States that it [the Northwest Passage] be under the control of Canada."

Resolving the Northwest Passage dispute will not be easy, but the Canadian government should be seizing the opportunity created by Cellucci. It's time for a two-pronged approach to the Northwest Passage dispute. First, we need proactive diplomacy to persuade the United States to recognize our claim and, in the interim, to identify avenues for cooperation, confidence building and contingency planning. Second, and concurrently, we need to take concrete steps to increase Canada's presence and capabilities in the Northwest Passage. As Donat Pharand told the Standing Senate Committee on Fisheries and Oceans, "The United States will never agree to recognize our full control over those waters unless they know that we have the capability to exercise that control, which we do not have at the moment." From a U.S. perspective, Canadian sovereignty combined with a lack of enforcement capacity might be worse than a waterway that was wide open to all. In an international strait, the United States could at least exert a military presence and, on the basis of the inherent right of self-defence, interdict vessels posing an imminent threat to itself or its citizens.

MUDDLING THROUGH IS NOT AN OPTION

Some experts believe it would not be in Canada's interest to press our Northwest Passage claim. Franklyn Griffiths argues that Ottawa and Washington could just muddle through, disagreeing on the law but cooperating on the practicalities of North American defence and economic development. Indeed, he suggests, the United States' willingness to acquiesce in a de facto increase in Canadian control—a consequence of the greater concern for home-land security and continental defence offsetting the historical need for naval mobility in distant regions—might be undermined by an attempt to open negotiations on the matter, since this would be to "pick a fight with the U.S. Navy." Griffiths even posits that:

> [T]hird parties are unlikely to challenge Canada over the enforcement of Canadian environmental and other laws on for-eign commercial vessels in the Archipelago. The third party that took Canada to the World Court would offer a challenge not only to Canada, but also the U.S. This it would do in threat-ening to breach the North American security perimeter by urging an adjudication that ran an international strait through the northernmost part of the continent.

This is an optimistic view, for a number of reasons. First, ris-ing temperatures and energy prices seem destined to make the Northwest Passage an important shipping route, with all the envi-ronmental and security challenges this will bring. Second, the U.S. Navy is sometimes amenable to changing its positions, as demon-strated by the fact that it now supports U.S. ratification of the UN Convention on the Law of the Sea. Third, it is not clear that all third parties will engage in complex calculations of U.S. interests or defer to them. Our neighbours and allies might be willing to cooperate while agreeing to disagree, but what about North Korea or al Qaeda? Fourth, adjudication is not the only way that Canada's position could be lost. We also need to ask whether the United States and other countries would look the other way if Canada interdicted a cargo ship flying a flag of convenience that entered the Passage without permission. Just a handful of protests, particularly from countries with special interests in the Arctic, could seriously damage Canada's claim.

Other experts argue that the status of the Northwest Passage is not so important because, even if it were an international strait, Canada already enjoys all the rights and privileges needed for responsible stewardship. There are several strands to this argument, all of which are problematic. First, it is sometimes suggested that, although Canadian jurisdiction within the Northwest Passage may be limited by the international straits regime, that jurisdiction is not so limited in the approaches to the waterway—where the full force of Article 234 of UNCLOS and the Arctic Waters Pollution Prevention Act applies. However, as Suzanne Lalonde pointed out to me, this suggestion conflicts with the official U.S. government position that "transit passage also applies in the approaches to international straits." It also seems inconsistent with common sense, since the right of transit passage within an international strait would be rendered meaningless if a different, more stringent legal regime applied to the approaches.

Second, the argument sidesteps the question of whether Article 234 will apply to waters that, while once ice-covered for most of the year, are progressively rendered ice-free for many months on end. There is nothing in Article 234 to suggest that waters subject to greater pollution prevention jurisdiction because they are covered with ice for most of the year retain that status if and when the ice disappears for lengthy periods. In other words, the rights accorded under Article 234 are not vested in the strait itself on an indeterminable basis but flow from the character of the ocean's surface there.

Third, the argument does not address the issue of whether Article 234 allows Canada to interdict a vessel that is non-compliant with the Arctic Waters Pollution Prevention Act or whether enforcement powers are restricted to the period after a pollution incident occurs. One international expert, Mary George, goes so far as to argue that "transit passage cannot be interfered with and...appropriate enforcement measures cannot be imposed on user States when in breach of a strait State's pollution regulations."

Canada's Northwest Passage claim is on thin ice, literally and figuratively. It's time to explore all our options, which include talking with the United States.

A MODEL NEGOTIATION

The widespread assumption that the U.S. position on the Northwest Passage is immutable may explain why the Canadian government failed to follow up on the opportunity created by Ambassador Cellucci in 2004. Indeed, it was not until August 2007 that Canada stepped forward—abruptly and at the highest of levels—when Stephen Harper reminded George W. Bush about Cellucci's views. Without any preparatory diplomacy, the news fell on deaf ears.

A few months later, I contacted Cellucci, who is now practising law in Boston, and suggested that a "model negotiation" might help delineate a path for official diplomacy. He agreed, and in February 2008 we met in Ottawa, backed up by two teams of the best non-governmental experts we could find. Our goal was to discuss the issues, identify possible solutions and make joint recommendations aimed at both governments.

We began by agreeing that government-to-government negotiations were urgently needed because increased northern shipping will be accompanied by greater security and environmental risks. We agreed that the long history of U.S.-Canada cooperation in the Arctic indicates the potential for bilateral agreement, as does the history of cooperation on shipping through other waters under national jurisdiction, such as the St. Lawrence Seaway. We negotiated nine concrete recommendations, which are reproduced in full in Appendix ii of this book.

Essentially, we recommended that:

1. The U.S. and Canada collaborate in developing parallel rules, standards and cooperative enforcement mechanisms for notification and interdiction zones in the northern waters of both Alaska and Canada.

2. The U.S. and Canada share maritime surveillance in northern waters and cooperatively develop further surveillance capabilities.

3. The two countries build on Canada's already strict Arctic marine environmental protection laws by developing even more advanced navigation, safety and ship construction and operation standards. (This recommendation accepts the legitimacy of applying the Arctic Waters Pollution Prevention Act to the Northwest Passage and seeks to improve upon the Act's standards. Indeed, all nine recommendations raise the bar with respect to environmental and safety protections without compromising Canadian sovereignty.)

4. The United States and Canada cooperate on the establishment of shipping lanes, traffic management schemes and oil spill response plans for the northern waters of both Alaska and Canada.

5. The two countries cooperatively address the immigration and search-and-rescue concerns arising as a result of the increasing number of cruise ships entering Arctic waters.

6. Both Canada and the United States acquire new state-of-the-art icebreakers to replace their aging coast guard vessels. (The

Harper government's announcement of $720 million for a new polar icebreaker came, probably coincidentally, just seven days after it received our recommendations.)

7. The two countries develop safety infrastructure—including navigation aids and perhaps even new port facilities—in support of northern shipping.

8. Canada and the United States make maximum use of the considerable legal powers they already possess over vessels, either those sailing to or from Canadian or U.S. ports or those registered in one or the other country.

9. A U.S.-Canada Arctic Navigation Commission be formed following the model of the International Joint Commission, which deals with transboundary fresh water issues.

Although we initially tried during the model negotiation to reach a consensus regarding the underlying legal dispute, it soon became evident that this would not happen in the two days available to us. However, those present did agree that the U.S. government should seriously examine the arguments in favour of recognizing Canada's legal position. Everyone involved in the model negotiation was convinced that the consequences of climate change in the Arctic require serious attention, increased cooperation and, ultimately, a legal reconciliation between North America's two Arctic nations.

At times, the negotiation was hard fought. Former ambassador Cellucci is also a former Republican governor who counts George W. Bush among his good friends. He and I are not natural allies. But arguably our political differences made the model negotiation all the more convincing as a demonstration of how Canadians can constructively engage Americans on the difficult issue of the Northwest Passage.

The model negotiation also highlighted the importance of demonstrating Canada's commitment to make the Northwest Passage a safe and secure international shipping route. Without our showing that we are up to that job, there is little reason for anyone to recognize our internal waters claim.

BUILD AN ARCTIC GATEWAY FOR THE WORLD

The Stephen Harper government has committed $1 billion to the Pacific Gateway Initiative, a series of infrastructure investments stretching across Canada's four western provinces. Capitalizing on the country's geographic location, the plan aims to develop the most efficient and secure transportation corridors possible between North America and Asia. Now, it is time for the next step. It is time for an Arctic Gateway Initiative.

Churchill, Manitoba, is currently the only commercial deep-water port in northern Canada. Climate change has already extended the shipping season there; it now runs from July to November. Long used for shipping grain to foreign markets, Churchill is beginning to see two-way trade. In October 2007, a Russian vessel arrived with fertilizer from Estonia and left with wheat for Italy.

OmniTRAX, the company that owns the port and the rail-line south, is pushing the concept of an Arctic Bridge from the Russian port of Murmansk through Churchill and on into the United States. The prime minister came on board in October 2007, promising $24 million in federal funds to provide upgrades for the port and railway.

But $24 million is chump change compared with the $1 billion provided for the Pacific Gateway Initiative. New highways, bridges and railway overpasses are being built across the Lower Mainland of B.C. A new container terminal is under construction at Prince Rupert, the Trans-Canada Highway through Banff National Park is being fully twinned, and new road interchanges are being built in Edmonton, Saskatoon and Winnipeg.

Why isn't the North part of this ambitious plan? It is not as if Harper has been ignoring the Arctic. But promises to strengthen

Canada's military presence there do little to promote trade and economic development.

An Arctic Gateway Initiative would embrace the North as a transportation opportunity. All-season roads would be pushed through to Tuktoyaktuk, Bathurst Inlet and Baker Lake. Deep-water ports would be built near the mouth of the Mackenzie River, and at Bathurst Inlet and Iqaluit. The Canadian Coast Guard would be charged with developing safe, commercially attractive, all-season shipping routes through the Canadian Arctic. This work would involve maintaining navigation devices and producing detailed charts. It would also, critically, involve breaking ice for commercial vessels—including foreign ones. The Coast Guard already breaks ice for cargo ships in the Gulf of St. Lawrence and the Saguenay River during the winter months. A new icebreaker in Hudson Bay could add months to the shipping season at Churchill. Additional icebreakers could ensure safe transits for commercial vessels through the Northwest Passage, initially for three or four months, and before long throughout the year.

Arctic hubs for the transportation of goods to and from North America would relieve pressure on Vancouver, Prince Rupert, Halifax and Montreal. They would create jobs and spur economic development, not just locally but across the country, too. Most significantly, as Donat Pharand pointed out two decades ago, breaking ice for foreign vessels in the Northwest Passage would cement Canada's claim to sovereignty there. What cargo ship is going to refuse the offer of a safe, cost-effective transit on the basis that it does not want to ask Canada's permission to sail through?

Arctic sovereignty is only partly about using it or losing it. It is also about ensuring that when foreign ships enter Canada's Arctic, they do so on our terms. Let's give other countries an incentive to work with us. Let's build an Arctic Gateway for the world.

Chapter Six

Who Owns the Seabed?

"THE ARCTIC IS RUSSIAN." With four simple words, Artur Chilingarov, who led the expedition that planted a titanium Russian flag on the ocean floor at the North Pole, commanded global media attention in August 2007.

Observers of Russian politics took the assertion with a large grain of salt. They knew that Chilingarov was a member of the Russian Duma, in the midst of an election campaign. As Russian Foreign Minister Sergei Lavrov later explained, the flag plant was just a publicity stunt and had not been approved by the Kremlin. Lavrov compared the flag plant to the 1969 U.S. moon landing, and he was right to do so. Descending 4,000 metres below the thick, shifting ice of the Arctic Ocean is a technological feat that, at the moment, no other country could match. And like the U.S. astronauts who planted a flag on the moon, the Russian scientists were not, in fact, claiming sovereign territory.

But Canadian Foreign Minister Peter MacKay had already taken the bait. "Look, this isn't the fifteenth century," he exclaimed. "You can't go around the world and just plant flags and say, 'We're claiming this territory.' Our claims over our Arctic are very well established." MacKay's statement obscured the fact that Canada has never claimed the North Pole and that just two years earlier Canadian soldiers had flown to Hans Island to plant a Canadian flag.

Like their Russian and Danish counterparts, generations of Canadian politicians have learned that Arctic sovereignty is good election fodder. But Arctic sovereignty is never just a domestic issue; it also involves relations with other, often much more powerful countries. Playing the sovereignty card badly can have a negative impact on seemingly unrelated global matters that are sensitive and vitally important—such as nuclear disarmament talks between Russia and the United States. The negative impact can be magnified since journalists tend to pay more attention to confrontation than to cooperation. Chilingarov's and MacKay's comments led to a rush of excited reporting about an upcoming conflict over Arctic resources. Some headlines portrayed a North that was teetering on the brink of war.

In a deliberate response to all the misreporting, the Danish government invited the foreign ministers of the other four Arctic Ocean countries to Ilulissat, Greenland, in May 2008. The summit culminated in the Ilulissat Declaration, in which all five states reaffirmed their commitment to working together within an existing framework of international law. "We have politically committed ourselves to resolve all differences through negotiations," explained Danish Foreign Minister Per Stig Møller. "And thus we have hopefully, once and for all, killed all the myths of a 'race to the North Pole.' The rules are in place. And the five states have now declared that they will abide by them."

CANADA'S MOON MISSION: THE EXTENDED CONTINENTAL SHELF

Considerable excitement has been generated by U.S. Geological Survey reports that the Arctic might contain as much as 83 billion barrels of oil and 44 trillion cubic metres of natural gas. However, as noted in Chapter 1, the 2009 report indicated that most of the projected

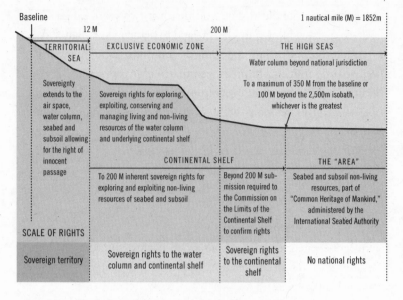

Baseline		1 nautical mile (M) = 1852m

12 M		200 M		
TERRITORIAL SEA	**EXCLUSIVE ECONOMIC ZONE**		**THE HIGH SEAS**	
			Water column beyond national jurisdiction	
Sovereignty extends to the air space, water column, seabed and subsoil allowing for the right of innocent passage	Sovereign rights for exploring, exploiting, conserving and managing living and non-living resources of the water column and underlying continental shelf		To a maximum of 350 M from the baseline or 100 M beyond the 2,500m isobath, whichever is the greatest	
	CONTINENTAL SHELF			**THE "AREA"**
	To 200 M inherent sovereign rights for exploring and exploiting non-living resources of seabed and subsoil	Beyond 200 M submission required to the Commission on the Limits of the Continental Shelf to confirm rights		Seabed and subsoil non-living resources, part of "Common Heritage of Mankind," administered by the International Seabed Authority
SCALE OF RIGHTS				
Sovereign territory	Sovereign rights to the water column and continental shelf	Sovereign rights to the continental shelf		No national rights

Jurisdictional Zones under the Law of the Sea

reserves are located in waters less than 500 metres deep. While this makes them accessible to drilling, it also means that they will probably be located on the continental shelf—and therefore within the uncontested jurisdiction—of one of the Arctic Ocean coastal states.

Unlike the Antarctic, a continent surrounded by oceans, the Arctic is an ocean surrounded by continents. For this reason, it is governed in large part by the "law of the sea"—the body of unwritten but nevertheless binding rules of customary international law that were codified into the 1982 UN Convention on the Law of the Sea. So far, 158 countries have ratified this so-called constitution of the oceans, including four of the five Arctic Ocean states: Canada, Denmark (Greenland), Norway and Russia. The remaining Arctic Ocean country, the United States, accepts the key provisions of UNCLOS as customary international law. The U.S. is also expected to ratify the Convention shortly, its concerns about the national security implications of accepting limits on the freedom of the seas having been superseded by concerns about terrorism and shipments of WMD.

As discussed, under the law of the sea each coastal state has a 12 nautical mile (22 km) territorial sea. Each state also has an Exclusive Economic Zone (EEZ) from 12 to 200 nautical miles (370 km) offshore where, as the name suggests, it holds exclusive rights over the natural resources of the water column, ocean floor and seabed. A parallel rule accords coastal states sovereign rights over resource exploitations on their adjoining continental shelves, the relatively shallow areas of ocean floor alongside most land masses. By the early 1980s, it had become clear that new technologies and higher prices would eventually lead to the exploitation of oil and gas reserves more than 200 nautical miles from shore. As a result, Article 76 of UNCLOS specifies that coastal states may claim rights over an "extended continental shelf," beyond the EEZ, if the depth and shape of the seabed and the thickness of underlying sediments indicate a "natural prolongation" of the shelf closer inshore.

Article 76 is one of the most technical provisions found in any international treaty. It essentially establishes two possible approaches for identifying the limits of an extended continental shelf and allows a state to use them in combination. Both require scientists to determine the location of the "foot of the continental slope," which is where the descending shelf flattens out and transitions into the abyssal depths.

The first approach is based on the ratio between the thickness of the sediments and the distance from the foot of the slope. Simply put, the continental shelf ends when the thickness of the sediments drops below 1 per cent of the shortest distance to the foot of the slope. The second approach involves a straightforward measurement of 60 nautical miles in a seaward direction from the foot of the slope. The coastal state can choose which of the two approaches to use with respect to *any given point* along its outer limit, and the state will invariably select the combination of approaches that extends its rights farthest out.

Provided that either or both of these approaches show a continental shelf extending beyond 200 nautical miles, Article 76 imposes two maximum limits: either 350 nautical miles from shore, or 100 nautical miles beyond the point where the depth of the water reaches 2,500 metres. Again, the coastal state can choose whichever limit or combination of limits works best for it.

Countries are supposed to submit their claims and supporting scientific evidence to the UN Commission on the Limits of the Continental Shelf within ten years of ratifying UNCLOS. The commission, which is made up entirely of scientists elected by the ratifying states, does not respond with binding decisions. Instead, it makes recommendations that, because they are based on geographic and geological facts, are treated as having considerable weight. When Moscow filed a claim to an extended continental shelf in 2001, the commission responded by asking for more data, and Russian scientists have been busily mapping the Arctic Ocean ever since, with a view to making a revised submission in 2013. In 2009, the commission responded favourably to Norway's submission, which included parts of the Arctic Ocean seabed north of the Svalbard Islands but did not approach any zone that Canada might claim.

None of this should concern anyone. The sheer size of the Arctic Ocean and the lengths of uncontested coastlines mean that Russia might legitimately claim an expanse of seabed larger than Europe. Canada, with the world's longest coastline, might be able to claim an area larger than two prairie provinces. Countries that do not border on the Arctic Ocean might feel left out, but because UNCLOS applies globally, most have the opportunity to make the same kinds of claims along their coastlines.

Apart from the technical exercise of collecting and assessing the scientific evidence, the only issue concerns possible overlaps between claims. Overlaps can occur where there are disputed maritime boundaries closer inshore, since the dividing line beyond 200 nautical miles is usually simply an extension from the starting point. As outlined later in this chapter, Canada has disputes of this kind with the United States in the Beaufort Sea and Denmark in the Lincoln Sea. A mid-ocean overlap is also possible between the Canadian, Russian and perhaps Danish claims along the Lomonosov Ridge, an undersea mountain range that bisects the Arctic Ocean north of Ellesmere Island and Greenland.

The North Pole itself is located in 4,000 metres of water well off to the side of the Lomonosov Ridge. The Pole is unlikely to form part of any natural prolongation and will instead fall within the "common heritage of mankind"—a technical term used to designate those deep seabed areas (collectively referred to as the "Area") that are beyond national jurisdiction and are administered by the UN. Yet a great deal of money and effort will be spent trying to establish that the North Pole is part of one or another country's extended continental shelf, if only for reasons of nationalistic pride and domestic politics. If hydrocarbons should be present at such depths, the cost of accessing them would be prohibitive. And an extended continental shelf provides no rights whatsoever to the ocean surface or any resources located in the water column itself.

The UN commission will not make recommendations with regard to any overlaps between claims. It is up to the countries involved to negotiate a solution, refer the matter to an international court or arbitral tribunal, or simply agree to disagree and not issue exploration licences for the contested area. Another possibility is the negotiation of a joint development regime whereby two or more countries share any royalties.

For two decades after UNCLOS was adopted, the Canadian government made little effort to map the Arctic Ocean seabed. Then, when Canada made the decision to ratify the convention in 2003, not enough attention was paid to the ten-year timeline for filing an extended continental shelf claim. In 2004, the federal budget allocated $70 million for seabed mapping. Only half of that was designated for the Arctic—this to map an area of seabed roughly the size of Alberta and Saskatchewan combined, located thousands of kilometres from any Canadian port, subject to some of the most extreme weather conditions on earth as well as total winter darkness, and impenetrable to all but the most powerful icebreakers. To give just one example of the costs, an icebreaker in heavy ice consumes up to $100,000 of fuel per day.

At least Canada's diplomats and scientists understood the challenges. As Ruth Jackson of the Canadian Geological Survey explained in March 2006, "We're making a claim for posterity. This is a one-chance opportunity." Faced with having to conduct the equivalent of a moon mission on a shoe-string, these people turned for help to other countries, beginning with Denmark.

In March 2006, a Canadian-Danish team set out with helicopters and ski-planes to determine whether the Lomonosov Ridge is part of the same geological structure as Ellesmere Island, or as that of Greenland, or perhaps that of both islands. Hundreds of seismic sensors and depth charges were lowered through the ice. When the explosives were detonated, shock waves bounced off the ocean floor and off layers of sediments and bedrock up to 40 km below the ocean floor, providing detailed geographical and geological information.

The next year, a Canadian scientist joined Danish scientists who had chartered two icebreakers—one Swedish, one Russian—to conduct a seismic survey north of Greenland. The Canadian government paid the operating costs of the ships for a few days, allowing for data collection in an area of particular interest to Canada. Then, in early 2009, another joint Canadian-Danish expedition took measurements from the ice surface, while a specially modified DC-3 aircraft flew 40,000 km collecting gravitational and magnetic information about the underwater geology.

Canadian scientists have also begun working closely with their American colleagues, as was displayed during the summer of 2008 when two red ships sailed in tandem through the northern Beaufort Sea. Leading the way was the U.S. icebreaker *Healy*, which cleared a path so that the Canadian icebreaker *Louis S. St. Laurent* could use its sensitive seismic equipment to map the sediments of the seabed. Then, when the noise produced by the breaking of particularly thick ice interfered with the seismic equipment, the ships switched positions. This allowed state-of-the-art sonar equipment on the *Healy* to be used to map the ridges and valleys of the ocean floor. The *St. Laurent* took over the task of opening a path.

Although the United States has not yet ratified UNCLOS, it clearly intends to do so soon, and it might even make an early submission to the UN Commission on the Limits of the Continental Shelf. In these circumstances, there is every incentive for the two countries to cooperate: both stand to benefit, and each possesses just one suitable icebreaker for a task that requires two. In the summer of 2009, the two icebreakers returned to the northern Beaufort Sea for another six weeks of mapping.

The benefits of the cooperation may be substantial. "The quality of the data is astonishing," Jacob Verhoef of the Canadian Geological Survey said in November 2008. "We haven't analysed it all, but what we found is that the entire Beaufort Sea—all the way up to the north—is covered with significant amounts of sediments, which makes our case look very promising." Verhoef was referring to the approach to identifying the outer limits of a continental shelf that involves a ratio between the thickness of the sediments and the distance to the foot of the slope. The Mackenzie River has been carrying massive quantities of sediments into the Beaufort Sea for millions of years, and that may have created a situation where Canada's sovereign rights extend a very long way offshore.

Unfortunately, most of us will not find this out until at least 2013, because the scientific partnership between the *Louis S. St. Laurent* and the *Healy* has been marred by an excessive concern for confidentiality on the part of the Canadian government. In a strange difference of approach, the information obtained by Canada has been kept secret, while the U.S. data are posted on the Internet. An agreement concluded between the Canadian and U.S. governments allows data collected by the U.S. vessel to be published, while data collected by the Canadian ship are kept out of the public domain.

The United States has a long-standing policy of promptly releasing seabed data, and not just from its icebreakers. Oceanographic observations collected by submarines are also made public, including data that were acquired during the Cold War. When operational circumstances permit, naval submarines will even travel to specific locations to gather data at the request of civilian scientists.

The Canadian government used to release its oceanographic observations. But a cloak of secrecy has now descended upon Canada's seabed mapping, enveloping both seismic surveys conducted through the sea-ice and data from the *Louis S. St. Laurent*. It is a nonsensical change of policy. Submissions filed by Canada, the United States and other countries should be based on common data sets that reflect the most complete, and therefore most accurate, scientific understanding of the seabed. Concealing data will not change the sediments and shape of the seabed, but it might engender suspicion about Canada's methods and motives.

The cooperation with the United States on mapping should also be extended into the development of mutually supportive submissions, which would ideally be filed at the same time. Doing so would dramatically increase the chance of the UN Commission endorsing both claims. But before this can happen, Ottawa and Washington will have to resolve their maritime boundary dispute in the Beaufort Sea—since that line provides the starting point for the boundary between their respective claims to an extended continental shelf.

Then there is Russia, which ratified UNCLOS in 1997 and filed a preliminary submission just four years later. The submission encroached on areas that Canada, Denmark and the United States hope to claim for themselves, but it also expressly envisaged negotiating overlaps with them. As mentioned, Canadian scientists relied on a Russian icebreaker to help with seismic mapping north of Greenland in September 2007. Three months later, Stephen Harper and then Russian Prime Minister Viktor Zubkov signed an agreement that recognized "the need for cooperation and collaboration in the mapping work in the Arctic Ocean, particularly since such work necessitates the collection of data under the most extreme and adverse weather conditions."

In February 2009, Alan Kessel, the senior lawyer in Canada's Department of Foreign Affairs, met with his Russian counterpart, Roman Kolodkin, in Moscow. According to a Russian summary of the meeting, the two men discussed the possibility of a joint Russian-Canadian-Danish submission to the UN Commission, thus resolving the issue of the Lomonosov Ridge in advance between the three countries. Delivering on this possibility—and, ideally, including the United States in the joint submission—would be a diplomatic coup that could ensure peace and cooperation in the Arctic for decades to come. It should be pursued with all deliberate speed—and with the full support and engagement of the Canadian prime minister.

It is not clear that the Canadian government understands the urgency. In August 2007, Jacob Verhoef warned the unpredictability of Arctic ice conditions meant that the tightly scheduled mapping plan depended on everything going right: "If anything goes wrong, and we lose one or two field seasons—which we very likely will because of conditions in the Arctic—we are in trouble." In February 2008, the federal government allocated an additional $20 million for Arctic seabed mapping, but it also began to consider the possibility of filing an interim claim—or perhaps even just a notice of intent to file—when the deadline arrives in 2013. If the government takes this approach, Canada, a member of the G8, will join a number of developing countries that were unable to meet their deadlines.

The choice the Canadian government makes, between joining a group of developing countries by filing late, or leading a joint submission from three or even four Arctic Ocean states, will speak volumes about its view of Canada's role in the world.

THE BEAUFORT SEA

The Beaufort Sea is that shallow portion of the Arctic Ocean located between Alaska and the Canadian Arctic Archipelago, just to the north of the Mackenzie River delta. Seismic surveys and exploratory wells have established that the seabed sediments there contain oil and gas comparable with that of Prudhoe Bay, Alaska—the largest oil field in North America—located just 300 km to the west. In 2006, Devon Canada discovered a potential 250 million barrels of oil north of Tuktoyaktuk, a small Inuvialuit community in the Northwest Territories. The next year, Imperial Oil and ExxonMobil Canada paid $585 million for exploration rights over a nearby area of seabed. Then, in 2008, BP paid $1.2 billion for rights in an area adjacent to the Imperial-Exxon-Mobil leases.

With these amounts of money being spent, the issues are not so much whether the oil and gas is there, but when the market price will justify its extraction, how it will be moved to market, and what to do with an unexplored 21,436 km^2 pie-shaped sector located directly northeast of the land border between Alaska and the Yukon Territory. Both Canada and the United States claim the sector, in a dispute that did not become apparent until Washington protested the boundary line that Ottawa was using when issuing oil and gas concessions in 1976. The existence of the dispute was confirmed the following year, when both countries delineated exclusive fishing zones out to the 200 nautical mile limit—and used different lines.

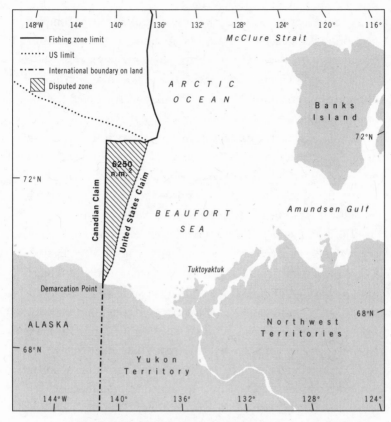

The Beaufort Sea / SOURCE: DAVID H. GRAY

Canada's position on the Beaufort Sea boundary is based on an 1825 treaty between Russia and Britain. The United States took on Russia's treaty rights when it purchased Alaska in 1867; Canada assumed Britain's rights in 1880. The treaty sets the eastern border of Alaska at the "meridian line of the 141st degree, in its prolongation as far as the frozen ocean." Canada claims that the maritime boundary, like the land border, must follow the 141°w meridian straight north.

At least three arguments are made in Canada's favour. First, the historic reason for the 1825 treaty was to establish spheres of maritime influence, with the land border being added for completeness only. As a result, the treaty's application to the maritime boundary in the Beaufort Sea is consistent with the treaty's "object and purpose." Object and purpose is one of the guiding principles of treaty interpretation, both in customary international law and in the 1969 Vienna Convention on the Law of Treaties.

Second, the authentic text of the 1825 treaty is in French and, in that language, the preposition "*jusqu'à*" in the phrase "*dans son prolongation jusqu'à la Mer Glaciale*" would normally be interpreted as inclusive of the object to which it relates. In other words, in French, "as far as the frozen ocean" includes the ocean.

Third, similar wording was used to define the maritime boundary in the Bering Strait and the Chukchi Sea in the 1867 Treaty of Cessation of Alaska to the United States. In 1990, the United States and the Soviet Union accepted and updated the 1867 treaty using the 168° 58' 37"w meridian "into the Arctic Ocean as far as permitted by international law." As Professor Camille Antinori of the University of San Francisco has observed: "The United States is virtually saying that the same treaty that delimits a maritime boundary in the west does not delimit a maritime boundary in the east."

Lawyers being lawyers, all three of these arguments have been countered—including with the apt observation that nineteenth-century diplomats would not have envisaged the existence of sovereign rights beyond 3 nautical miles from shore.

Canada's position is complicated by the fact that, during the early twentieth century, it used the 141st meridian in conjunction with the sector theory to define its jurisdiction all the way to the North Pole. As explained in Chapter 3, Canada's attitude toward the sector theory later shifted to studied ambiguity, until Stephen Harper definitively abandoned the theory in 2006. As a result, it has become more difficult to argue that early invocations of the sector theory were also, concurrently, unopposed expressions of Canada's preferred interpretation of the 1825 treaty.

Canada's position is further complicated by the fact that international law tends to treat each maritime boundary dispute as distinct, even when similar geographic, legal and political issues are in play. This makes it more difficult to argue that the United States is bound to Canada's position in the Beaufort Sea just because it accepted a meridian to delimit the boundary with Russia. However, as Professor Ted McDorman of the University of Victoria explains, that acceptance in western Alaska does at least indicate "what the United States might consider an equitable result" in eastern Alaska.

Equity is, in fact, a central component of the U.S. position, which holds that "as far as the frozen ocean" means the boundary follows the 141st meridian only as far as the coast. Offshore, Washington argues that a general principle of equity requires that every point on the boundary be an equal distance from each of the two adjacent coasts. Since the coast of Alaska, the Yukon and the Northwest Territories slants east-southeast from Point Barrow, Alaska, to the mouth of the Mackenzie River, such an "equidistance line" would give more of the ocean and seabed to the Americans. This is why, on a map, the disputed area looks like a southward-pointing wedge.

For more than three decades now, the two countries have treated the matter with restraint. In the mid-1980s, Canada issued two exploration licences that included part of the disputed zone and immediately made them subject to work prohibition orders. In 1997, David Gray of the Canadian Hydrographic Service reported that Canada and the United States had "established a moratorium on exploration" in the contested area. More recently, Washington has held several auctions for oil and gas leases in the zone, and Ottawa has responded with diplomatic protests. No bids were received, reportedly because oil companies were concerned about the unresolved boundary.

Ultimately, the oil companies will determine when the dispute is resolved. As more of the Beaufort Sea is explored, the multinationals will eventually turn their attention to the contested sector and demand legal certainty. The U.S. government, which is intent on developing secure supplies of energy, can be expected to respond.

Canada has always taken the view that some sort of compromise is possible. This view is strengthened by the fact that Canadian companies such as EnCana are already operating, under U.S. licences, in the uncontested U.S. portions of the Beaufort Sea. It is entirely conceivable that the same companies will obtain leases in the contested area once the legal situation is resolved. For better or worse, Chapter Six of the North American Free Trade Agreement created a common energy market between Canada and the United States and thus reduced the significance of sovereign jurisdiction over hydrocarbons. The extremely low royalty rates that will likely be accorded to Arctic offshore drilling also operate in favour of a compromise, since they reduce the potential financial losses associated with any concession.

A compromise could take several forms. The first is a negotiated boundary, perhaps one that divides the disputed zone into two identically sized portions. Anything less might be difficult to sell to voters, not just in Canada but also in Alaska, were the United States to end up with the smaller portion.

A second option is for the two countries to send the dispute to an international court or arbitration tribunal. This approach off-loads the responsibility onto lawyers, judges or arbitrators, and it has the dubious attraction of delaying the result past one or more elections. However, third-party dispute settlement is not risk-free. In 1903, Canadians were dismayed by an arbitration award that gave all 26,000 km^2 of the Alaska Panhandle to the United States. That outcome, and the fact that it was a British-appointed arbitrator who cast the decisive vote, prompted the creation of an independent Canadian foreign ministry in 1909. More recently, U.S. fishers were upset when the International Court of Justice gave part of the Georges Bank to Canada in the 1984 *Gulf of Maine Case*.

A third option is a joint development regime for energy resources in the disputed zone—a relatively unusual approach that has worked before, including in the Arctic. In 1981, Norway and Iceland concluded a treaty giving Norway the right to 25 per cent participation on a portion of Iceland's continental shelf between that country and the Norwegian Island of Jan Mayen. In 2008, the two countries adopted a follow-up treaty setting out the framework for cooperative oil and gas exploration in the zone. According to the Norwegian minister of Foreign Affairs, Jonas Gahr Støre, the treaty provides the predictability that oil companies need. Other joint development regimes exist between Australia and East Timor and between Thailand and Malaysia.

As Ted McDorman explains, Canada and the United States "could either agree to set aside the boundary issue and share the exploration costs and development benefits of any hydrocarbon resources in the disputed area; or proceed with a maritime boundary but have a joint zone for hydrocarbon activity, the benefits of which would be shared by both States." During negotiations over both the Beaufort Sea and the Gulf of Maine in 1977, both countries agreed in principle to use the latter approach. But they lost interest in the matter after deciding to send the Gulf of Maine dispute to the International Court of Justice.

Today, any settlement of the Beaufort Sea dispute would have to include the Inuvialuit of the northern Yukon and the Northwest Territories. The contested zone falls within the Inuvialuit Settlement Region, which was established by the 1984 Inuvialuit Final Agreement on the basis of the Canadian position concerning the international boundary. Specifically, the disputed sector is located in an area known as the Yukon North Slope, where a special conservation regime protects wildlife and aboriginal harvesting interests.

A fourth option is a trade, whereby one country's position is accepted in one boundary dispute, in return for the other country's position being accepted in another dispute. In September 2008, polar expert Willy Østreng reported that Norway and Russia were about to agree on a trade related to two border disputes in the Arctic. According to Østreng, Russia would accept Norwegian fisheries jurisdiction around the Svalbard Islands in return for Norway accepting a more westward dividing line for the continental shelf in the Barents Sea. There is also some reason to believe that Norway's 1930 recognition of Canadian sovereignty over the Sverdrup Islands was tied to Britain's recognition of Norwegian sovereignty over Jan Mayen. Scott Borgerson of the U.S. Council on Foreign Relations, who participated in the February 2008 model negotiation described in Chapter 5, has suggested that Canada should lay all its Arctic issues on the table to achieve a "grand compromise" with the United States, thus linking the Beaufort Sea boundary to the resolution of the Northwest Passage dispute.

Another trade might be facilitated by the fact that, nearly 2,000 km away, Canada and the United States have a boundary dispute that involves one of the world's richest salmon fisheries. The dispute is at the very southern end of the Alaska Panhandle, where the 1903 arbitration tribunal drew the boundary line along the north shore of the Dixon Entrance, a 50-kilometre-wide body of water that connects the mainland coast to the open sea. Canada claims that the line set both the land and the maritime boundary, and that the entire Dixon Entrance consequently belongs to this country. The United States claims that the line forms the land border only and that the maritime boundary must be delimited on the basis of equity, dividing the Dixon Entrance more or less equally. If the U.S. claim prevails, Canada will lose 2,746 km^2 of prime fishing grounds.

A friendly exchange, whereby Ottawa recognized Washington's claim in the Beaufort Sea in return for Washington's recognizing Ottawa's claim in the Dixon Entrance, would provide certainty for both countries and clarity of jurisdiction for their energy and fishing industries. That only one U.S. state would be affected should simplify negotiations, along with the fact that each country's national pride could remain intact.

Unfortunately, the Canadian government is now considering whether to leave the Beaufort Sea dispute unresolved when it submits its claim to an extended continental shelf with the UN. The thinking is that, because the Commission on the Limits of the Continental Shelf will not make recommendations with respect to disputed areas, Canada could simply ask the commission to stay away from the disputed zone and continue with the status quo. But such an approach would simply delay the inevitable. It would also negate the opportunity for creative trade-offs involving multiple disputes, and it would stall the momentum of the recent, very positive cooperation on seabed mapping.

THE LINCOLN SEA

The Lincoln Sea is that portion of the Arctic Ocean located directly to the north of Greenland and Ellesmere Island. The Arctic's thickest sea-ice is found there, pushed into the space between the two islands and held in place for years by prevailing winds and ocean currents. The negotiators who delimited the boundary between Canada and Greenland in 1973 stopped when they reached the point where Nares Strait opens into the Lincoln Sea. As a result, the nearly 200 nautical miles of continental shelf (and later EEZ) boundary to the north was left unresolved.

In 1977, Canada claimed a fisheries zone in the Arctic Ocean. That zone was bounded in the east by a Lincoln Sea boundary that was based on the equidistance principle, using the low-water line of the coasts and several fringing islands as reference marks. Not to be outdone, Denmark drew straight baselines around Greenland three years later. But unlike Canada's claim, the Danish baselines use 10 km² Beaumont Island as a reference point. This has the effect of

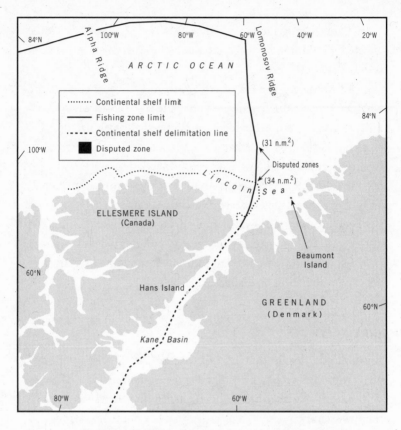

The Lincoln Sea / SOURCE: DAVID H. GRAY

pushing the equidistance line slightly westward, adding two iso-lated, lens-shaped areas of 105 km^2 and 115 km^2 to the Greenland side.

Canada immediately objected to the baselines, probably for four reasons derived from the 1951 *Anglo-Norwegian Fisheries Case*: (1) Beaumont Island is somewhat west of the other islands and thus not part of a fringe of islands; (2) the baselines are overly long; (3) they do not follow the general direction of the coast; and (4) they do not cross the mouths of the intervening fjords but are farther offshore. However, Canada undermined its position in the Lincoln

Sea when it drew its own straight baselines around the Canadian Arctic Archipelago in 1986. As we saw in Chapter 3, those baselines proved controversial, for reasons that include their unusual length and their possible departure from the general direction of the coast.

The Lincoln Sea dispute has no implications for the delimitation of Canada and Denmark's extended continental shelves in the Arctic Ocean beyond 200 nautical miles, because the two lens-shaped disputed areas are located closer than that to shore. The dispute could easily be solved, with one option being to split the difference. Canada and Denmark could each take one of the lens-shaped areas. If uncertainties about hydrocarbon potential made this an unpalatable option, the two countries could agree to share any revenues eventually obtained from areas thus assigned. Or they could declare two condominiums subject to shared sovereignty and a joint hydrocarbon exploitation regime—though given the small size of the disputed areas, this last option seems impracticable.

An innovative solution would be to connect the Lincoln Sea dispute with Canada's efforts to obtain international recognition of its position in the Northwest Passage.

Canada's straight baselines were protested by the European Commission on behalf of all the member states of the European Community (now the European Union). For this reason, Denmark is on record as opposing the very same baselines that the Mulroney government drew in 1986 to strengthen Canada's Northwest Passage claim. As Chapter 3 explains, the waters landward of straight baselines are "internal waters," subject to the full control of the coastal state—provided that other countries acquiesce to the baselines.

Russia is the only country that has supported Canada's position in the Northwest Passage. And while it is nice to have the backing of one Arctic Ocean country, adding another would bolster our claim. For this reason, one possible compromise would be for Canada and Denmark to accept each other's straight baselines. Canada would lose its claim to 220 km² in the Lincoln Sea but would gain diplomatic and legal support for its position in the Northwest Passage. That said, the issue of whether the Northwest Passage was an international strait *before* Canada drew the straight baselines would not be affected by Danish recognition, unless Copenhagen could be persuaded to explicitly address that point.

Conceivably, the United States might seek to dissuade Denmark from recognizing Canada's straight baselines. The United States has a longstanding relationship with Denmark that includes the presence of an important airbase and radar station at Thule, Greenland. However, it might be possible to prevent or overcome pressure from the United States by engaging in parallel negotiations with Washington on the Northwest Passage (as discussed in Chapter 5) or, perhaps, sweetening the pie by adding the possibility of full sovereignty over Hans Island to the negotiating mix. Whether Ottawa could convince the Canadian public of the benefits of Danish recognition of the straight baselines and the irrelevance of Hans Island is, perhaps, another matter.

Chapter Seven

Sovereignty and the Inuit

"CANADA HAS A choice when it comes to defending our sovereignty in the Arctic: either we use it or we lose it." Stephen Harper's July 2007 statement was bold and succinct, but it did not impress Lorne Kusugak. "What the hell is he talking about?" the mayor of Rankin Inlet, Nunavut, asked me. "We've been using 'it' for thousands of years, and we're not going anywhere."

The feeling of chagrin is heaviest in Canada's two northern-most communities. The Inuit call Resolute Bay "Qausuittuq" (the place where the sun never sets) and Grise Fiord "Auyuittuq" (the place where the ice never melts). These Inuktitut names reflect the fact that, historically, the Inuit did not live this far north.

The Canadian government's decision to relocate seventeen families to the Queen Elizabeth Islands in 1953 and 1955 was moti-vated by concerns about possible Danish or American claims. The Inuit, whom government officials identified by numbers rather than their names, were essentially treated as flag poles. They were subsequently utilized as a resident source of cheap labour for RCMP detachments and at the Royal Canadian Air Force Base at Reso-lute Bay. There was, to be fair, some talk about the need to relieve the overpopulation of Inukjuak, the source Inuit community in northern Quebec. But if the interests of the Inuit were paramount, why move people more than 1,500 km northward to a High Arctic desert that bore little resemblance to their home?

There were reasons why the Inuit had not lived that far north before. Resolute Bay is an expanse of frozen gravel swept by persistent and powerful winds. Even in June, a stroll along the shoreline left me wishing that I had brought my parka along. For the Inuit, it was like landing on the moon. Their traditional knowledge and hunting techniques were out of place, there was not enough snow to build igloos, and the total darkness from November to February was both unfamiliar and disabling.

Tuberculosis added to the misery. Those who survived the first few winters did so by scavenging food from the Air Force dump or bartering their bodies. The survivors call themselves the High Arctic exiles, and they include some of the Inuit's most influential leaders. John Amagoalik, the Father of Nunavut, was five years old when he was relocated. So too was Martha Flaherty, who later became the president of Pauktuutit, the Inuit Women's Association. Senator Willie Adams, then a teenager, had the foresight to jump ship at Churchill, Manitoba, during his intended relocation.

In 1996, more than forty years later, the Canadian government finally agreed to a $10 million compensation package. But it ignored the recommendations of three different bodies—the House of Commons Standing Committee on Aboriginal Affairs and Northern Development, the Canadian Human Rights Commission and the Royal Commission on Aboriginal Peoples—by refusing to apologize. The refusal was described by Amagoalik as a "real slap in the face for us."

Although the compensation agreement recognized Inuit "pain, suffering and hardship," it also stated that "government officials of the time were acting with honourable intentions in what was perceived to be the best interests of the Inuit." The Inuit who signed the 1996 agreement felt they were doing so under duress. Their overriding concern was for the financial well-being of the surviving elders, who were running out of time.

Much has happened since 1996. Climate change has vaulted Arctic sovereignty to the top of Canada's agenda, prompting, as we have seen, a series of promises designed to strengthen our military presence in the North. But the prime minister has failed to consult or cooperate with the Inuit, as was unfortunately illustrated when he ignored Inuit views on the appropriate site for an Arctic port and chose uninhabited Nanisivik over Iqaluit. Insult was added to the injury when Harper failed to invite Premier Paul Okalik to the announcement in Resolute Bay, failed to stop in Iqaluit on his way back to Ottawa, and even failed to mention the Inuit in his speech. As John Amagoalik later told the Standing Senate Committee on Fisheries and Oceans, "That's not going to work."

The Inuit know the clock cannot be turned back. They want to work with other Canadians to forge a better future. They seek to preserve the Arctic environment, to protect our common sovereignty, and to provide their children with a quality of life equivalent to that in the rest of Canada. But the Inuit also want respect. For a prime minister who really cares about sovereignty, apologizing to the High Arctic exiles would be an excellent next step.

UPHOLDING THE BARGAIN

One of my favourite photographs was taken by Doug Struck of the *Washington Post* in Igloolik, Nunavut, during our 2006 Northwest Passage voyage aboard the *Amundsen*. It shows a Canadian Coast Guard helicopter parked along the shore, with a little Inuit boy sitting inside, smiling and dangling his feet out the open door. I have shown the photograph to thousands of people across Canada, told them it concerns sovereignty, and asked why this might be so. Almost everyone focusses on the bright red helicopter, for what more tangible demonstration of the Canadian government's presence could one hope for in the North? In fact, the little boy is more important to Canadian sovereignty than is any aircraft or icebreaker, since it is he and his ancestors who have provided us with the most morally and legally compelling component of our claim.

In August 2007, I met with Paul Kaludjak, the president of the Inuit land claims organization Nunavut Tunngavik Inc. He told me how, in the 1993 Nunavut Land Claims Agreement, the Inuit transferred their claim to aboriginal title over one-fifth of Canada's area. In doing so, they explicitly sought to strengthen the country's sovereignty there. It was the Inuit negotiators who suggested the inclusion of a paragraph that reads: "Canada's sovereignty over the waters of the Arctic archipelago is supported by Inuit use and occupancy."

As discussed in Chapter 3, the ability of nomadic peoples to acquire and transfer sovereignty rights was affirmed by the International Court of Justice in the 1975 *Western Sahara Case*. However, any argument based on a transfer of rights is weakened if the recipient fails to uphold the bargain, or to address other basic grievances held by the transferees. And the Canadian government made a number of commitments in the Nunavut Land Claims Agreement that have not yet been fulfilled. For instance, Article 23 requires that the percentage of government jobs held by Inuit match their share of the population. Today, the Inuit account for 85 per cent of the population in Nunavut—and hold only 45 per cent of the jobs.

In 2005, Thomas Berger, the former B.C. Supreme Court judge and sole commissioner in the 1974–1977 Mackenzie Valley Pipeline Inquiry, was engaged as a conciliator by the federal government, the territorial government, and Nunavut Tunngavik Inc. In March 2006, he identified that the main impediment to equitable employment was the 25 per cent high school graduation rate among Inuit children. The root cause of this was the language of education. In most of Nunavut, Inuktitut is the language of instruction from kindergarten through Grade 4. It is then abandoned completely in favour of English-only education from Grade 5 onward. At this point, according to Berger:

> Inuit children are starting over, and they find themselves behind. Their comprehension is imperfect; it slips and as it does they fall further behind. By the time they reach Grade 8, Grade 9 and Grade 10, they are failing (not all of them, to be sure, but most of them). This is damaging to their confidence, to their faith in themselves. For them, there has been not only an institutional rejection of their language and culture, but also a demonstration of their personal incapacity. The Inuit children have to catch up, but they are trying to hit a moving target since, as they advance into the higher grades, the curriculum becomes more dependent on reading and books, more dependent on a capacity in English that they simply do not have. In Nunavut this reinforces the colonial message of inferiority. The Inuit student mentally withdraws, then leaves altogether.

Berger concluded that the situation demands a fully bilingual Inuktitut-English education system from kindergarten through Grade 12. Although this would cost a considerable amount of money, Berger said, boosting the number of Inuit in government jobs would "save tens of millions of dollars per year in costs such as those associated with the recruitment, hiring, and training of non-Inuit (mostly imported at considerable further expense from the South) for the same positions." It would also prevent untold social costs, which impose their own economic costs over time.

The education crisis is accompanied by a housing crisis, as was poignantly explained to me by Elisapee Sheutiapik, the mayor of Iqaluit. A burgeoning population, high construction costs, inadequate funding and federal foot-dragging have created a situation in which as many as fifteen to twenty people are crowded into small, poorly ventilated homes. Imagine how difficult it is for a child to do homework under such circumstances. Consider the health and social consequences, including astonishingly high rates of tuberculosis, lung cancer, depression and domestic violence. The overcrowding may explain why the HINI virus ("swine flu") has hit Inuit communities particularly hard.

Although some new federal money has recently been allocated, including $100 million for affordable housing in Nunavut, Mary Simon, the president of the national Inuit organization Inuit Tapiirit Kanatami, was right to call the amount "disappointing." Far more support will be needed to end the housing crisis in the North, from which so many other problems flow.

In communities across Nunavut, I have witnessed the problems affecting Inuit youth, including depression, drug and alcohol abuse and a truly disturbing suicide rate. In a twelve-month period in 2006–2007, fifteen young men killed themselves in Kugluktuk, a hamlet of just 1,500 souls in western Nunavut. Just think about it: as a result of the suicides, Kugluktuk is losing its young men to violence at a rate comparable to that in some of the world's worst conflict zones.

Nunavut is Canada's largest, most remote and most impoverished region, all of which makes the provision of health and social services difficult and costly. If Nunavut were independent, it would be the twelfth largest country by area on earth. Similar challenges exist in Nunatsiavut (Labrador), Nunavik (northern Quebec), the Inuvialuit Settlement Region (Northwest Territories and Yukon) and much of the rest of the Canadian Subarctic.

Adding to the pressure is the profound cultural change exemplified by the abrupt transition from dogsleds and igloos to Boeing 737s and the Internet, in just two or three generations. Now, as a result of climate change, people's highways and hunting grounds—the frozen tundra and the sea-ice—are literally melting away. In the circumstances, it's easy to understand why so many Inuit have mental and physical health problems.

There is incredible human potential in the North. As Thomas Berger observed, "Every Canadian must be aware of Inuit achievements in art and sculpture, in film and performance arts, achievements for which the Inuit have won international renown. The Inuit are a bright tile in the Canadian mosaic."

I have witnessed the strong protective instinct that the Inuit have for the flora and fauna of the North. I've sung "O Canada" in Inuktitut with one hundred school children in Cambridge Bay and felt their deep love for this country. I've participated in a community feast in Rankin Inlet and watched the elderly and the poor given first choice of the wide selection of "country food." I've met community and territorial leaders of intelligence and integrity, all of whom have a clear sense of all that Nunavut could, and must, be. There is so much that can be done—with foresight, a relatively small amount of money, and a genuine effort to listen and cooperate.

In 2007, I met with Paul Okalik, then premier of Nunavut, who told me how his government's request for a deepwater wharf at Iqaluit, the largest community in the territory, had just been rebuffed by Ottawa. By facilitating the off-loading of construction supplies, fuel oil, gasoline and dry goods, such a wharf would help reduce the prohibitive cost of living in the North. A deepwater wharf would also attract cruise ships, many of which currently bypass Iqaluit, thus enhancing the development of Nunavut's tourism and artisan industries.

The federal government could also do more to ensure that the Inuit benefit from the exploitation of natural resources within Nunavut. For decades, the now closed lead-zinc mine at Nanisivik employed many Inuit men; today, Baffinland mining company is taking a similar approach at its Mary River iron ore mine. The company is even reaching out to the next generation of workers, as I discovered in June 2008 when a planeload of school children from Igloolik crowded into the tiny one-room airport at Nanisivik.

They were on their way home from a field trip to Mary River when Igloolik became fogged in. Unfortunately, most of those kids will never graduate from high school, let alone university, which means they will never advance beyond operating machinery or cleaning toilets. The lack of a fully bilingual Inuktitut-English education limits Inuit access to the private sector, too.

The Royal Canadian Mounted Police have at least two constables in every northern community and are, to their credit, training and employing some Inuit officers. This helps to bridge the linguistic and cultural divides that can impede law enforcement, while helping to redress a history of misbehaviour among some of the young white men sent north. The Standing Senate Committee on Fisheries and Oceans has recommended that the Coast Guard should likewise actively recruit Inuit—for what could better reinforce the contribution of Inuit use and occupancy to Canada's Northwest Passage claim than having Inuit officers and sailors crew Canadian icebreakers?

Many Canadians know about one important form of Inuit employment—namely, the Canadian Rangers. The program helps with search-and-rescue and cold-weather training, but one of its other functions is to provide part-time jobs and a sense of pride and purpose for thousands of young men who would otherwise not be part of the wage economy.

However, most of the opportunities for further economic and social development in the Arctic will depend upon infrastructure that is currently either non-existent—like a port at Iqaluit—or creaking at the seams. In Pangnirtung, Mayor Manasa Evic explained to me how successive federal governments have ignored pleas to extend or, ideally, move the hamlet's runway. The present airstrip is less than 1,000 metres long, close to a steep hillside, and in close proximity to houses, fuel tanks and a school. The mayor also told me of his community's campaign for a small-vessel harbour to enable fishing boats to off-load their catches directly on shore. This would greatly improve safety while reducing costs at the local fish plant, a thoroughly modern facility that prepares and packages shrimp, turbot and Arctic char for the U.S. market, employing up to forty Inuit.

The federal government has recently promised $25 million for development of the harbour at Pangnirtung, but other communities such as Pond Inlet, Clyde River and Qikiqtarjuaq are desperate for similar facilities, and their calls have not been answered. And though the first $8 million for Pangnirtung was announced in February 2008, it took until May 2009 before a request for tenders for the first stage—steering the project through the federal government's own environmental approval process—was published.

At Rankin Inlet, the municipal and territorial governments have been working with Manitoba on a plan to build a 400-kilometre-long transmission line to bring hydro power north from Churchill. Yet the plan, which would eliminate the need to ship in large quantities of diesel fuel, has hit a brick wall in Ottawa. An even more ambitious plan involves building a road to Churchill and southward from there to Manitoba's existing road network. The governments of Nunavut and Manitoba shared the cost of a feasibility study from the engineering company snc-Lavalin that set the price tag for the 1,200-kilometre route at $1.2 billion. That's a lot of money to spend up front, but over time the road would likely pay for itself through reduced shipping costs and increased economic activity. More than a century ago, a Canadian government built a railway to create a country that stretched from sea to sea, but is the same kind of vision present in Ottawa today?

Dennis Bevington, the mp for the Northwest Territories, would like to see communities across northern Canada use wind power to reduce their reliance on expensive, polluting diesel. Although wind power developed a bad reputation in the Northwest Territories and

Nunavut during the 1990s when several pilot projects failed, new hybrid wind-diesel technologies are proving much more successful and reliable in the Yukon and Alaska. But, despite the dogged efforts of the New Democrat MP, the federal government has shown little interest in supporting wind power in the North, or anywhere else in Canada. Now, the NWT government is pushing ahead on its own by funding the installation of four wind turbines at Tuktoyaktuk. Serving a community of just 900 people, the turbines are projected to provide 20 per cent of their electrical needs and save 88,000 litres of diesel annually.

Iqaluit is an obvious location for wind power in Nunavut. Strong and steady winds sweep over a diesel power plant located on the large hill above town, sometimes wafting fumes into the streets and the homes of seven thousand people. Massive storage tanks line the shores of Frobisher Bay, waiting for tankers to replenish them each summer with diesel refined in Quebec or New Brunswick from oil produced in the Middle East. It is both an environmental disaster and a shameful waste of money, yet a territorial government that is almost entirely dependent on federal transfer payments cannot afford to remedy the problem on its own.

Sometimes, it would make enough of a difference for southern decision-makers just to consider the needs and interests of Canadians living in the North. A recent example involves the reallocation of fishing quotas in Baffin Bay, offshore from the Inuit communities of Pangnirtung, Qikiqtarjuaq, Clyde River and Pond Inlet. In January 2008, Loyola Hearn, the federal minister of Fisheries and Oceans, was asked by Nova Scotia's Seafreez Foods to approve the transfer of its quotas to two other companies based in the Atlantic provinces. Hearn agreed, ignoring pleas for some of the quota from two small Inuit-owned companies that were already engaged in the fishery (using ocean-going trawlers they purchased and crewed) and eager to expand.

Working with the Inuit, investing in social programs, building infrastructure, creating economic opportunities—all of these things are important from a fairness perspective, since northern Canadians are as entitled to Ottawa's support as the rest of us. But they are critically important for another reason, too.

As outlined in Chapter 2, the Inuit have been central to Canada's sovereignty claims since 1930, when the federal government invoked Inuit interests to deny a Norwegian request for commercial access to the Sverdrup Islands. In 1986, the proclamation of straight baselines around the Canadian Arctic Archipelago was justified partly on the basis that these were consolidated by Inuit use and occupancy. When I speak about the Northwest Passage at universities and foreign ministries around the world, the thousands of years of Inuit use and occupancy of the sea-ice is the only dimension of our legal position that resonates with non-Canadians.

The Inuit are, however, becoming increasingly frustrated with the federal government. In December 2006, after Stephen Harper's newly elected government refused even to meet with conciliator Thomas Berger, Nunavut Tunngavik Inc. launched a lawsuit aimed at forcing Ottawa to uphold its obligations under the Nunavut Land Claims Agreement. The federal Department of Justice has spent millions of dollars fighting the case on every conceivable ground. And by so doing, it is putting Canada's legal position in the Northwest Passage at risk.

Inuit leaders see a clear connection between Canadian sovereignty and the Nunavut Land Claims Agreement. Indeed, Paul Kaludjak of Nunavut Tunngavik Inc. told the Standing Senate Committee on Fisheries and Oceans: "We are now in court because the Government of Canada has failed to implement an agreement which, given full force and effect, would strengthen Canada's Arctic sovereignty." Some Inuit are so upset with the federal government that they are even discussing the possibility of withdrawing support for Canada's claim. It is not a step the Inuit want to take, given the environmental risks that would flow from the Northwest Passage becoming an international strait. But the mere fact that the possibility is being discussed should set off alarm bells in southern Canada. We cannot take the Inuit for granted: if we wish to maintain their support, we have to keep our promises.

John Amagoalik describes the Nunavut Land Claims Agreement as the Inuit's "entrance into Confederation." As Arctic expert Terry Fenge explains, implementing the agreement is "an ongoing expression of a negotiated partnership between the Government of Canada and the Inuit of Nunavut and could be an important component of a strategy to assert, affirm and express Canada's Arctic sovereignty."

Fenge is correct: Canada should be thinking about how to strengthen the Inuit dimension of our Northwest Passage claim. Hiring Inuit in the Coast Guard is one way; another is to devolve some of the federal government's existing powers to Nunavut and give it the status of a province.

In international law, as noted, the term "internal waters" refers to those maritime areas located within straight baselines that are subject to the full control of the coastal state. "Internal waters" also have a particular status in Canadian domestic law. In the 1984 *Georgia Strait Reference*, the Supreme Court of Canada was asked about the status of the seabed between Vancouver Island and mainland British Columbia. The court held that, since the western boundary of the Colony of British Columbia was the Pacific Ocean off the west coast of Vancouver Island, the waters to the east belonged to the colony. British Columbia kept the same boundaries when it joined Canada and became a province, which means that the seabed under those "internal waters" belongs to B.C.

The same is true on the Atlantic coast, where Canada has drawn a straight baseline across the mouth of the Gulf of St. Lawrence between Newfoundland and Nova Scotia. In 2002, Nova Scotia and Newfoundland asked an arbitration panel to delimit the maritime boundary between their respective jurisdictions in the internal waters created landward (i.e., to the west) of the straight baseline. The same kind of provincial rights would, logically, flow to Nunavut once devolution to provincial status was achieved.

Before becoming prime minister, Stephen Harper promised that the three northern territories would be the primary beneficiaries of natural resource revenues in any devolution deal with a Conservative government. Although it took three years, progress toward such a deal has now begun. In September 2008, the federal minister of Indian Affairs and Northern Development met with the premier of Nunavut and the president of Nunavut Tunngavik Inc. The three of them—Chuck Strahl, Paul Okalik and Paul Kaludjak—signed a Devolution Negotiation Protocol.

The preamble to the Protocol recognizes that "the Inuit of Nunavut are largely a coastal people who have a deep attachment to both the land and the marine areas of Nunavut." It makes reference to the 1993 Nunavut Land Claims Agreement, which "gave the Inuit of Nunavut certain specific rights and responsibilities in respect of Inuit Owned Lands and a role in the territory's overall resource management regime."

More pointedly, the Protocol specifies: "The parties acknowledge that it is the position of the GN and NTI that the ultimate objective of devolution is the transfer of administration and control in respect of Crown lands and resources in all areas, both onshore and in the seabed." It also specifies: "The parties further acknowledge that it is the position of the GN and NTI that a devolution agreement should make no distinction between resource management regimes onshore and in the seabed in and adjacent to Marine Areas."

None of this implies that the federal government agrees with the position of the Government of Nunavut and Nunavut Tunngavik

Inc. Even if it did, the Protocol is non-binding. The Protocol also explicitly postpones the issue of the seabed: "The parties acknowledge that, owing to, among other factors, the need of the GC to consider national consistency and coherency in seabed resource management, the GC is not prepared to negotiate seabed resource management during the initial phase of devolution negotiations." The parties did, however, agree "to discuss the management of onshore and seabed oil and gas resources as an integrated unit in a future phase of devolution negotiations."

The fact that discussions are taking place is a step toward strengthening Canada's sovereignty. As Suzanne Lalonde has concluded, devolving rights over the seabed within the Archipelago would, by reinforcing the role of Inuit use and occupancy, carry weight in international law:

> Devolution of legislative jurisdiction over the land resources and marine bed resources in the Territory of Nunavut to its Government could be a further and important exercise of Canada's exclusive authority over the waters of the Arctic Archipelago. Particularly should such action draw no notice or protests from foreign governments, it would undoubtedly strengthen Canada's claim under the historic waters doctrine.

Recognizing Inuit control of oil and gas resources would also facilitate the development of Nunavut's economy and generate much-needed income for the Government of Nunavut. The territorial government faces monumental challenges in providing basic services to thirty thousand people scattered across one-fifth of Canada without having its own tax and royalty base.

At the moment, the plight of the Inuit undermines the credibility of Canada's Northwest Passage claim, since it is not as if other countries are unaware of the hypocrisy of holding forward Inuit use and occupancy as a central component of our legal position while allowing the same people to suffer so badly. The Inuit have given us all that they have, in pursuit of a quintessentially Canadian dream. It is time for the rest of Canada to reciprocate—to help the Inuit realize their, and by extension, our, new national vision.

INTERNATIONAL INFLUENCE

The Inuit's role in international diplomacy extends beyond their contributions to Canada's sovereignty claims. The Inuit Circumpolar Council, an international organization that draws the Inuit of Alaska, Canada, Greenland and Russia together into a unified political force, has proven itself an international actor of consequence. In the 1990s, the ICC played a decisive role in the negotiation and adoption of the Stockholm Convention on Persistent Organic Pollutants. These toxic chemicals, which include DDT and PCBs, were produced and mostly used in the industrialized regions of the world. Disproportionate amounts were, and still are, being carried to the Arctic by a process of global distillation involving volatilization at low latitudes and condensation at high latitudes, also known as the "grasshopper effect." After being deposited in the Arctic, these toxins move up the food chain, accumulating in the fatty tissues of predators such as seals, bears and ultimately humans.

One of Canada's most effective politicians, Sheila Watt-Cloutier, represented the Inuit during the negotiation of the Stockholm Convention. Throughout the negotiations, she made a point of educating everyone involved about the fact that the Inuit are the world's most affected victims of persistent organic pollutants, to the point where Inuit women should think twice about breastfeeding their babies. During a particularly critical stage in the talks, Watt-Cloutier presented a soapstone carving of an Inuit woman and child to Klaus Toepfer, the executive director of the

United Nations Environmental Programme. Her efforts paid off: the Stockholm Convention, adopted in 2001, requires states to take specific steps to reduce or eliminate the production of persistent organic pollutants and to dispose safely of existing stocks. So far, 162 countries have ratified the convention, including Canada, China, the European Community, India and Japan. In May 2009, the Convention was amended to include nine new chemicals, some of which are still widely used as pesticides and flame retardants and will now be phased out.

The Inuit are also helping to alert southerners to the immediacy of the climate change crisis, something greatly facilitated by the fact that they are, collectively and individually, very much on the front line. Their traditional way of life has become more difficult, even dangerous, to sustain, as temperatures rise, weather patterns change, snow and ice conditions become less predictable, and populations of their food animals decline.

In 2005, Sheila Watt-Cloutier and sixty-two other Inuit from Canada and Alaska filed a petition with the Inter-American Commission on Human Rights in Washington, D.C. They argued that the United States, by failing to reduce its massive emissions of carbon dioxide and other greenhouse gases, has violated the cultural and environmental rights of the Inuit. Although the Commission declined to hear the petition for jurisdictional reasons, the effort was successful in raising media and public awareness about climate change in the United States. In 2007, Watt-Cloutier was a nominee for the Nobel Peace Prize in recognition of her work on international environmental issues.

The international influence of the Inuit is likely to grow as Greenland acquires more autonomy from Denmark and cooperates more closely with Nunavut. It is even possible to imagine an eventual federation of sorts between Greenland and Nunavut—perhaps following the model of the Mohawk nation of Akwesasne, which straddles the border of Canada and the United States—as the Inuit on both sides of Baffin Bay seek to increase their influence and benefit from economies of scale.

For the Inuit, cooperation and adaptation have always been prerequisites for survival. It took centuries of failed expeditions before European explorers learned to wear clothes made out of skins, eat seal blubber (which contains the Vitamin C necessary to prevent scurvy) and use dogs to pull sleds. That history has made it all the more difficult for Inuit leaders to accept their exclusion from inter-state negotiations, especially their exclusion from the summit of foreign ministers held in Ilulissat, Greenland, in May 2008.

One year later, in April 2009, the Inuit Circumpolar Council responded by issuing a declaration on sovereignty just a day before a summit meeting of Arctic Council foreign ministers in Tromsø, Norway. The declaration indicated a specific concern about the exclusion of the Inuit from the Ilulissat meeting:

> In spite of a recognition by the five coastal Arctic states (Norway, Denmark, Canada, USA and Russia) of the need to use international mechanisms and international law to resolve sovereignty disputes (see 2008 Ilulissat Declaration), these states, in their discussions of Arctic sovereignty, have not referenced existing international instruments that promote and protect the rights of indigenous peoples. They have also neglected to include Inuit in Arctic sovereignty discussions in a manner comparable to Arctic Council deliberations.

The declaration goes on to argue that the Inuit have rights as a people under international legal instruments such as the 2007 UN Declaration on the Rights of Indigenous Peoples. The argument overreaches a bit by failing to acknowledge that the UN Declaration is not a binding treaty, has not yet achieved the status of customary international law, and is actively opposed by the Canadian, New Zealand and U.S. governments. But the Inuit were right to conclude that "issues of sovereignty and sovereign rights in the Arctic have become inextricably linked to issues of self-determination in the Arctic. Inuit and Arctic states must, therefore, work together closely and constructively to chart the future of the Arctic."

John Amagoalik, as the former president of the Inuit Tapirisat of Canada, recalls attending a meeting at the United Nations where a foreign diplomat blithely stated that "nobody lived in the Arctic." Amagoalik approached the diplomat afterwards, held out his hand and said, "Hi, I'm nobody."

Another Amagoalik anecdote demonstrates even more poignantly the damaging disconnect between southerners and northerners. In 1969, he says, after the Canadian government failed to persuade Exxon and the U.S. government to request permission for the Northwest Passage voyage of the ss *Manhattan*, two Inuit hunters took matters into their own hands. As the super-tanker ploughed through the ice of Lancaster Sound, the two drove their dogsleds into its path. The vessel stopped, a short discussion ensued, and then the hunters—having made their point—moved aside.

The story is credible. The incident happened only four decades ago, and Inuit oral history is accurate over many generations. But the Canadian government, instead of using the incident to Canada's legal and diplomatic advantage, denies it ever occurred. "Nobody," it seems, was on the ice that day.

Conclusion

An Arctic for Everyone

ONE CLEAR ARCTIC night in the open waters of Foxe Basin, the crew of the *Amundsen* turned off the spotlights and sailed by the light of the aurora borealis and the stars. This enabled them to see farther into the distance as they scanned the waters for icebergs.

Standing on the darkened bridge, watching brilliant waves of silver, blue and green play across the heavens, I became acutely aware of our location on the curved surface of a tiny planet in the infinity of space.

Al Gore makes the point very powerfully in *An Inconvenient Truth*. Earth, with its wondrous balance of atmosphere, water, life and photosynthesis, is all we have. And through our stubborn, short-sighted addiction to fossil fuels, we are throwing that balance away.

The Arctic is in crisis. The ice and the permafrost—the foundations of its highly specialized ecosystems—are literally melting away, and with them the traditional way of life of the Inuit. A vast, ice-bound, impenetrable ocean is being transformed into a new Mediterranean Sea, a "middle sea" over which the world's powers will trade. Easier access and rising oil, gas and mineral prices will spark twenty-first-century gold rushes, challenging the political will and governance capabilities of governments who, for decades, have largely ignored the Arctic.

There is only one way to preserve the North in anything approaching its natural state, and that is to dramatically reduce greenhouse gas emissions in the South. Every Arctic-specific policy imperative, whether on sovereignty, security, shipping or search-and-rescue, is driven by the need to adapt to the increasingly severe consequences of climate change.

Climate change presents the ultimate collective action problem, what Garrett Hardin famously termed "the tragedy of the commons." With hundreds of governments, thousands of stateless transnational corporations and billions of consumers embroiled in a fossil fuel–based economy, opportunities abound for pursuing one's own gain at the expense of the common good. This makes stabilizing the atmosphere the most improbable cooperative exercise ever attempted by humankind. Yet there is no Plan B, no alternative planet to which we can collectively decamp. We simply have to cooperate.

The Arctic is one place to start: a vast, sparsely populated region with only a handful of nation-states; only a few, relatively minor boundary disputes; and a pre-existing framework of universally accepted international rules, centrally including the law of the sea. If humanity cannot cooperate in the Arctic, it cannot cooperate anywhere.

Seen from this perspective, Canada's Arctic policies take on global importance. In addition to its domestic responsibility to provide good government within our national boundaries, the Canadian government has a broader, overarching responsibility to pursue every opportunity for international cooperation. That's the only way to save all that we value, including right here at home.

Sovereignty and international cooperation are not incompatible. To the contrary, sovereignty can facilitate cooperation by providing clear jurisdiction for regulating shipping and the extraction of natural resources, and for guarding against non-state security threats. International law results from centuries of interstate cooperation, as countries have defined the boundaries between their respective jurisdictions *and* worked together in pursuit of common goals.

Resolving our disputes over Hans Island and the maritime boundary in the Lincoln Sea would set a positive course for Canadian diplomacy in the North and help cement important relationships with both Denmark and Greenland. Engaging the United States with respect to the maritime boundary in the Beaufort Sea would confirm that cooperative trajectory and provide useful elements for a larger compromise over the extended continental shelf. The same kind of proactive engagement is called for regarding the Northwest Passage, before it's too late.

Canadian politicians have to stop their bellicose rhetoric about Russia's actions, and the ongoing behind-the-scenes cooperation between Ottawa and Moscow should be publicly recognized. Working with the Russian government to resolve potential overlaps in our extended continental shelf claims, to regulate Arctic shipping and to provide search-and-rescue does *not* imply approval of that country's human rights record or of its actions in Chechnya and Georgia. In fact, working with Russia will contribute to a larger effort, led by U.S. President Barack Obama, to "push the reset button" on U.S.-Russia (and therefore NATO-Russia) relations. The importance of this contribution cannot be overstated. If Obama is successful in re-engaging Russia, both former antagonists will make deep cuts to their nuclear arsenals, leading to a much safer world for everyone.

From a purely legal perspective, five countries own parts of the Arctic, Canada prominent among them. In terms of international law, at least, we are an important Arctic nation. But the Arctic is not a box sealed off from the rest of the world. It is a human place, full of connections and emotions, where lives are lived and histories made. It is a laboratory for international cooperation across the historic fault-lines of the Cold War. And it is a place of critical natural importance, located on the front lines of the greatest crisis ever to have threatened this, our fragile Spaceship Earth.

In the end, the important question isn't "Who owns the Arctic?" It is instead "Are we, as a country, up to the task?"

A Northwest Passage Scenario

FINGERS CROSSED = SOVEREIGNTY LOST

"Shipping companies are going to think about this, and if they think it's worth it, they are going to try it. The question is not if, but when."

ALAIN GARIÉPY, CAPTAIN OF THE CCGS *AMUNDSEN*,
INTERVIEWED IN THE NORTHWEST PASSAGE BY
DOUG STRUCK OF THE *WASHINGTON POST*, OCTOBER 2006

TO RECAP, AS we saw in Chapter 3, Canada's sovereignty in the Northwest Passage has not been seriously challenged since the U.S. Coastguard icebreaker *Polar Sea* sailed through without seeking permission in 1985. Three years later, Brian Mulroney persuaded Ronald Reagan to sign a bilateral treaty on such voyages. The United States undertook to notify Canada before sending any icebreaker through, while Canada promised to provide its consent. This agreement-to-disagree removed U.S. icebreaker voyages from the legal dispute between the two countries.

At that point, with the ever-present ice preventing other kinds of vessels from using the Passage, Canada adopted a strategy of letting sleeping dogs lie. The hope was that, in the absence of further challenges to our sovereignty, the passage of time would gradually strengthen Canada's claim. The strategy failed to foresee the dramatic impact of climate change, however. Since 2006, the Northwest Passage has been ice-free every summer, making it probable that Canada's sovereignty will be challenged again, most likely by a commercial vessel.

The following scenario—developed in association with my students at UBC—demonstrates just how quickly sovereignty could be lost. Faced with this risk, it is imperative that Canada negotiate a new Northwest Passage treaty with the United States. In a rapidly changing, increasingly busy Arctic, the interests of both countries would best be protected by an acceptance of Canadian sovereignty, coupled with a renewed Canadian commitment to police and manage the waterway.

Log Entry, Maritime Forces Atlantic, Halifax, August 18

The *Lucia III*, a Panamanian-flagged container ship owned by Seascape, has provided the 96-hour notice required by the Marine Transportation Security Act for entry into Canadian waters.
CURRENT LOCATION: 30 nautical miles SE of Cape Sable, Nova Scotia.
ALL CARGO CHECKED AND CLEARED BY PORT OF ORIGIN: Newark, New Jersey.
SECURITY RISK: Low. No further action.

Blog Entry, Private Yacht Arctic Explorer, *August 23, Lancaster Sound, Nunavut*

Just had a close call! A massive container ship named the *Lucia III* almost ran us down. The ship is sailing west into the NW Passage with nobody on deck—and nobody answering the radio. Can't help but wonder whether they're supposed to be there. Will radio the Coast Guard at Iqaluit, just in case.

**E-mail, Canadian Coast Guard to Transport Canada
& Department of National Defence, August 23**

SUBJECT: Container ship in NW Passage
STATUS: Urgent

The private yacht *Arctic Explorer* (home port: Victoria, B.C.) reports a large container ship sailing west through Lancaster Sound toward Barrow Strait.

Vessel name: *Lucia III*. Home port: Panama City.

The ship has failed to provide notice under NORDREG, Canada's maritime registration system in the Arctic, as is recommended—but not yet required—under Canadian law.

The vessel has NOT responded to our efforts at radio contact.

Recommend satellite confirmation by RADARSAT-2 and visual contact by any government personnel on aircraft or vessels in vicinity.

Nearest Coast Guard vessel is the icebreaker *Terry Fox* assisting with a resupply mission to the weather station at Eureka, three days north of Lancaster Sound.

Please advise as to Canadian Forces assets.

**E-mail, Department of National Defence to Canadian Coast Guard
& Transport Canada, August 23**

SUBJECT: Re: Container ship in NW Passage
STATUS: Urgent

The *Lucia III* provided the 96-hour notice required by the Marine Transportation Security Act while off Nova Scotia on August 18.

In accordance with established procedures, voyages originating in U.S. ports are designated low security risks.

We will exercise our priority access and secure RADARSAT-2 imagery today.

Nearest CF vessel: HMCS *Charlottetown* is in Frobisher Bay for a sovereignty operation. Two days south of Lancaster Sound. Like other CF ships, the *Charlottetown* is not ice-strengthened. We are reluctant to send her west of Lancaster Sound because of the risk from any remaining sea-ice.

Nearest CF aircraft: Cormorant search-and-rescue helicopter at Gander, Newfoundland (16 hours away); Hercules fixed-wing at Trenton, Ontario (6 hours away). Plans to base a Cormorant at Resolute Bay during the summer months were shelved for budgetary reasons.

E-mail, Transport Canada to Department of National Defence & Canadian Coast Guard, August 24

SUBJECT: Re: Container ship in NW Passage
STATUS: Urgent

We have chartered a Twin Otter fixed-wing aircraft through the Polar Continental Shelf Project at Resolute Bay. An RCMP constable from the local detachment will accompany the pilots to provide official confirmation.

E-mail, Transport Canada to Foreign Affairs Canada, August 24

SUBJECT: Panamanian container ship in NW Passage
STATUS: Very Urgent

The Panamanian-flagged container ship *Lucia III* is currently in Barrow Strait heading west toward Prince William Strait or McClure Strait. Confirmation received from RADARSAT-2 satellite imagery and RCMP officer on chartered plane. No response to radio. No response to fly-by. No notice provided under NORDREG.

Weather conditions are good; all routes ice-free. The ship is likely to complete transit within next three days.

Please advise diplomatic status ASAP.

Briefing Note for Minister of Foreign Affairs, August 25

SUBJECT: Panamanian ship in Northwest Passage
SECURITY LEVEL: Canadian eyes only

The *Lucia III* is a 17,000-ton container ship owned by Seascape, a holding company incorporated in the Channel Islands. Actual ownership is unclear. The vessel itself is registered in Panama, a flag-of-convenience state.

The *Lucia III* set sail from Newark, New Jersey, on August 17 en route to Shanghai, China, with a load of mostly empty containers. The contents of the remaining containers were checked and cleared by the Port of Newark.

While still off Nova Scotia, the *Lucia III* provided the 96-hour notice required by the Marine Transportation Security Act before entering Canadian territorial waters. The voyage was deemed a low security risk because of the U.S. port of origin. No further action was taken.

However, the *Lucia III* failed to provide notice under NORDREG, Canada's northern shipping registration system. Canada's consent has not—repeat not—been sought for a NW Passage voyage.

According to the *Financial Times*, Seascape is on the brink of bankruptcy, as are many other shipping companies in the current economic crisis.

The decision to use the NW Passage was likely motivated by economic considerations.

The NW Passage is currently ice-free, including the entire deep-water route from Lancaster Sound through Barrow Strait, Viscount Melville Sound and McClure Strait. This information is widely available in media reports and on the Canadian Ice Service website.

For a voyage between Newark and Shanghai, the NW Passage offers a 7,000-kilometre shortcut, saving millions of dollars in time and fuel.

Lloyds of London indicates that the ship carries standard insurance only. The special insurance needed for a NW Passage voyage would be much more expensive. The lack of special insurance may explain the failure to register under NORDREG, since Canada could be expected to require such coverage before granting permission for the vessel to proceed.

But while requirements for higher insurance levels are explicitly foreseen in the Arctic Waters Pollution Prevention Act, they have not yet been implemented through regulations.

The *Lucia III* was built in South Korea in 1997 and may well meet the other, mostly safety equipment requirements of the Arctic Waters Pollution Prevention Act.

Nevertheless, a voyage that took place without Canada's consent would undermine our long-standing position that the NW Passage constitutes "Canadian internal waters."

The Panamanian flag is a particular concern. Panama makes a great deal of money providing a flag of convenience to international shipping companies. In return, those companies expect not only a relaxed regulatory regime but also a staunch defence of the freedom of the seas.

Time is of the essence. The vessel will likely leave Canadian waters in just two days.

We have limited assets in the region but could interdict the vessel using a long-range Canadian Forces search-and-rescue helicopter based in Newfoundland or southern B.C., or a Coast Guard icebreaker already in the Arctic.

In the circumstances, we request permission:

(1) To contact Seascape, confirm the voyage, and indicate that Canadian consent must be sought and would be granted—

provided that the company can confirm compliance with the safety equipment requirements. We could, in this instance, ignore the lack of special insurance because: (a) We have not issued specific regulations; and (b) Container ships pose less of an environmental risk than oil tankers.

(2) In the event that Seascape is unavailable or non-compliant, to contact the Government of Panama and request that it: (a) order the vessel to comply; and, if necessary, (b) give us permission to interdict. Securing flag-state cooperation would prevent any damage being caused to Canada's legal position, since only nation-states contribute to making or changing international law.

E-mail, Deputy Minister of Foreign Affairs to Clerk of the Privy Council, August 25

SUBJECT: Foreign Ship in NW Passage
STATUS: URGENT / TOP SECRET

The *Lucia III*, a Panamanian-flagged container ship, has entered McClure Strait en route to a completed Northwest Passage transit WITHIN THE NEXT TWO DAYS.

Canada's consent was NOT sought for the voyage, which could create a damaging precedent against our legal position.

Attempts to contact the registered owner of the vessel have failed. The Canadian Forces and/or Coast Guard are capable of reaching and interdicting the vessel before it leaves our waters.

The Government of Panama says it will protest any interference, on the grounds that the Northwest Passage is an international strait open to vessels from every country without constraint.

The Arctic Waters Pollution Prevention Act could be used as a basis to inspect the vessel. Since the adoption of the 1982 UN Convention on the Law of the Sea, the Act has been widely accepted as compatible with international law. But there is no reason to believe that the *Lucia* III fails to meet Canada's safety equipment standards or intends to dump waste in our waters.

Moreover, simply inspecting the vessel would NOT prevent a damaging precedent.

Arresting the vessel on the basis of inadequate insurance coverage just before it left Canadian waters would stretch legal and diplomatic credibility, especially since we have yet to issue regulations on Arctic-specific insurance requirements.

Our lawyers advise that Panama, in addition to protesting, could take Canada to the International Court of Justice in The Hague. Both countries have long accepted the court's "compulsory jurisdiction," meaning that either country can sue or be sued by any country that has also accepted compulsory jurisdiction. If the judges decided that the Northwest Passage is an international strait, we would have to accept the ruling.

In the circumstances, our best ally might be the United States. According to former U.S. ambassador Paul Cellucci, the State Department has been reassessing whether the traditional U.S. position—that the Northwest Passage is an international strait—remains in the U.S. national interest. The worry is that terrorists and other non-state actors might use an increasingly ice-free waterway to access North America and, potentially, traffic in WMD.

Panama is highly dependent on the United States and would likely accede to a request from it.

WE RECOMMEND that the Deputy Minister of Foreign Affairs contact the U.S. Under-Secretary of State to request immediate diplomatic pressure on Panama.

WE ALSO RECOMMEND that every effort is made to keep the situation SECRET. This will reduce the impact of the precedent, should the voyage proceed without Canada's consent.

SUBJECT: NW Passage

STATUS: URGENT / TOP SECRET

Prime Minister disturbed by news reports concerning Panamanian ship in NW Passage. Why wasn't the yacht *Arctic Explorer* asked to remove its blog entry? Do we have feedback from Washington?

SUBJECT: Re: NW Passage

STATUS: URGENT / TOP SECRET

The State Department cannot assist. The U.S. Navy is wedded to their traditional position that the NW Passage is an international strait. Although the State Department understands that an ice-free, legally unrestricted NW Passage could have negative consequences for U.S. national security, an inter-departmental agreement is impossible on short notice.

Among other things, they would need concrete commitments from Canada and a credible strategy for distinguishing the NW Passage from the other waterways they consider to be international straits.

Panama's foreign minister has just stated publicly that he will take us to the International Court of Justice if we interdict.

Although the vessel will leave Canadian waters in approximately 18 hours, interdiction is still an option. A Canadian Forces Cormorant helicopter from Comox, B.C., could get there in time, after several refuelling stops, but would be at the full extent of its range and far from any support.

The Canadian Coast Guard icebreaker *Louis S. St. Laurent* is a better choice. It is approximately 12 hours away, mapping the continental shelf in the northern Beaufort Sea. With two helicopters and light weapons on board, the crew is capable of interdicting—assuming there is no or only moderate resistance.

A peaceful outcome would be facilitated by sending one or more CF-18 fighter aircraft up from Cold Lake, Alberta, to do a fly-by during the interdiction. The Canadian Forces are keen to be involved in some way.

We thus face a dilemma:

(1) Arrest the ship, provoking diplomatic protests and probable litigation in the International Court of Justice; or

(2) Do nothing and wear the negative legal precedent that would result from our very public acquiescence.

Our lawyers advise that we have (at best) a 50-50 chance of prevailing before the International Court. They also advise that inaction would, given the now-widespread reporting of the situation, cause irreparable damage to our legal position.

The Prime Minister's Office may also wish to consider the domestic political consequences of being seen to "surrender" Canadian sovereignty. The "use it or lose it" rhetoric of the last few years makes inaction a difficult sell.

It may also be relevant that the International Court usually takes five to ten years before it issues a final judgement. Being taken to court might offer the benefit of postponing any ultimate loss of sovereignty until after the next election.

Recommendations:

(1) Order the *Louis S. St. Laurent* to proceed to the western entrance of McClure Strait and prepare for an interdiction.

(2) Obtain the Prime Minister's approval for an interdiction ASAP.

(3) In the future, avoid taking a "let sleeping dogs lie" approach with respect to issues of importance and risk. The State Department was coming around to our position and wanted to help. But we never gave them a chance. We should have engaged them proactively on possible concessions and strategies BEFORE the crisis arose.

My fellow Canadians, just one hour ago the men and women of the Canadian Forces and the Coast Guard engaged in bold and decisive action in defence of our Arctic sovereignty. A rogue cargo ship flying a flag of convenience was attempting to sail through the Northwest Passage without Canada's consent. This reckless act posed a security risk for Canada, the United States and all civilized nations. It also put the fragile Arctic environment at risk.

The ship is now in the capable hands of the Canadian Coast Guard. It will be released as soon as it has been sailed out of Canada's Arctic waters and 200-mile pollution prevention zone. The crew members are being held upon the Canadian icebreaker *Louis S. St. Laurent.* They are unharmed and will be treated respectfully in accordance with Canadian law.

I understand that some foreign governments may be concerned about our actions today. I say to them: Canada has acted reasonably and in full compliance with international law. We will never hesitate to defend our sovereign rights in the Northwest Passage, in the halls of international diplomacy and—if necessary—in court.

Model Negotiation
on Northern Waters

ON FEBRUARY 18 and 19, 2008, two teams of non-governmental experts met to discuss issues, identify possible solutions and make recommendations concerning navigation in northern waters to the governments of the United States and Canada. The following agreed-upon statement is the result of those deliberations.

AGREED RECOMMENDATIONS

Recognizing the rapid and dramatic loss of Arctic sea-ice;

Recognizing that this will increase the maritime accessibility of the Arctic;

Recognizing that increased shipping will bring many benefits, and that the development of economically efficient, environmentally responsible, safe and secure navigation in northern waters is in the interests of all countries;

Recognizing obligations under land claims agreements with indigenous peoples;

Concerned that increased shipping will bring heightened security risks, especially in the context of terrorism, nuclear proliferation, illegal immigration and drug smuggling;

Concerned that increased shipping will bring heightened environmental risks, especially in the form of oil spills and disruption of indigenous peoples and marine life;

Acknowledging the long history of U.S.-Canada cooperation, including within NATO, NORAD, the 1988 Arctic Cooperation Agreement, and the Arctic Council;

Acknowledging that the United States and Canada have previously cooperated to promote shipping through waters under national jurisdiction, namely the St. Lawrence Seaway, Great Lakes and Juan de Fuca Region, and that this has brought great benefits to both countries;

We respectfully recommend:

1. That the two countries collaborate in the development of parallel rules and standards and cooperative enforcement mechanisms with respect to notification and interdiction zones in the northern waters of Alaska and Canada;

2. The implementation of the 2006 expansion of the NORAD agreement, which includes the sharing of all maritime surveillance in the area covered by that agreement, and that the two countries cooperate in the development of further surveillance capabilities;

3. Building from the Arctic Waters Pollution Prevention Act, that the two countries develop common navigation, safety and ship operation and construction standards;

4. That the two countries cooperate on the establishment of shipping lanes, traffic management schemes and oil spill response in the northern waters of Alaska and Canada;

5. That the two countries cooperate with respect to immigration and search and rescue concerns related to cruise ships;

6. That the two countries accelerate the acquisition of new ice-breakers. The two countries should maximize burden-sharing opportunities, following the models of the U.S.-Canada ice-breaker agreement on the Great Lakes and the agreement on the resupply of Thule Air Base;

7. That the two countries step up their efforts to develop safety infra-structure, including search and rescue, in support of increased shipping in the northern waters of Alaska and Canada;

8. That the two countries make maximum use of their existing port state and flag state authority to promote safe, secure and environmentally responsible shipping.

We further recommend:

9. That the two countries consider establishing a U.S.-Canada Arctic Navigation Commission to address their common interests in navigation, environmental protection, security, safety, and sustainable economic development. This Commission should include representation from indigenous groups directly affected by navigation. This Commission would fol-low the model of the International Joint Commission by acting as a recommendatory body. This Commission should operate within the framework of the already legislated bi-national research body, the Arctic Institute of North America.

We reaffirm that the 1988 Arctic Cooperation Agreement has been very effective in managing the legal disagreement concerning the Northwest Passage, while *recognizing* the challenges presented by rapidly changing ice conditions.

Additionally, the Canadian team of experts presented strong arguments as to why the United States should recognize Canada's legal position that it controls the Northwest Passage. The changing Arctic environment raises new security concerns. In this context, the Canadian team argued that recognizing Canadian control of the Northwest Passage could substantially enhance North American security, without compromising U.S. interests elsewhere in the world. The U.S. team also pointed out that the U.S. position has strong arguments in its favour.

The two teams together *respectfully request*, without prejudice, that the U.S. and Canadian governments examine all of these arguments.

Finally, the two teams emphasize that time is of the essence and that the recommendations listed in Points 1 to 8 be addressed expeditiously.

*

THE MODEL NEGOTIATION was funded by ArcticNet, a federally funded consortium of scientists from twenty-seven Canadian universities and five federal departments. The International Joint Commission (Canadian Section) provided meeting space. The recommendations above represent the opinions of the team members, who were as follows:

U.S. Team

Paul Cellucci, U.S. Ambassador to Canada, 2001–2005
Scott G. Borgerson, Council on Foreign Relations
Professor Elizabeth Elliot-Meisel, Department of History,
     Creighton University
Professor Christopher Joyner, Department of Government,
     Georgetown University
Professor Eric Posner, University of Chicago Law School
Coalter Lathrop, J.D., President, Sovereign Geographic, Inc.

Canadian Team

Professor Michael Byers, Department of Political Science,
     University of British Columbia
Colonel (retired) Pierre Leblanc, Former Commander, Canadian
     Forces Northern Area

Aaju Peter, Inuit law student, Iqaluit
Professor Rob Huebert, Department of Political Science and Centre for Military and Strategic Studies, University of Calgary
Professor Ted McDorman, Faculty of Law, University of Victoria
Professor Suzanne Lalonde, Faculty of Law, Université de Montréal
Professor Armand de Mestral, C.M., Faculty of Law, McGill University

Secretariat

Justin Nankivell, PhD student, University of British Columbia
Joël Plouffe, PhD student, Université du Québec à Montréal

Notes

INTRODUCTION: ARE THE RUSSIANS COMING?

page 2 *a strong coincidence:* Steven Chase, "Ottawa rebukes Russia for military flights in Arctic," *Globe and Mail*, February 28, 2009.

page 3 *aggressive Russian actions:* Ibid.

page 3 *Russians have maintained compliance:* Ibid.

page 3 *let the record show:* Don Martin, "Peter's MacKay's Dr. Strangelove moment," *National Post*, March 3, 2009.

pages 3–4 *Serdyukov op-ed:* Anatoliy Serdyukov, "Don't demonize Russia," *National Post*, March 30, 2009.

page 4 *current headlines:* Ken Coates, Whitney Lackenbauer, William Morrison and Greg Poelzer, *Arctic Front: Defending Canada in the Far North* (Toronto: Thomas Allen, 2008), 215.

CHAPTER I: WHY SOVEREIGNTY MATTERS

page 8 *Circumpolar Inuit Declaration: A Circumpolar Inuit Declaration on Sovereignty in the Arctic*, April 2009, available at: http://www.itk.ca/circumpolar-inuit-declaration-arctic-sovereignty

pages 9–10 *undiscovered oil and gas:* Donald L. Gautier et al., "Assessment of Undiscovered Oil and Gas in the Arctic," (29 May 2009), 324 (5931), *Science*, 1175–79.

page 10 *five Arctic Ocean countries reaffirm commitment:* "The Ilulissat Declaration," Arctic Ocean Conference, Ilulissat, Greenland, May 27–29, 2008, available at: http://byers.typepad.com/arctic/ ilulissat-declaration-may-28-2008.html

page 11 *soon all sea-ice will melt during summer:* For the current situation, see the "Arctic Sea Ice News & Analysis" page at the U.S. National Snow and Ice Data Center: http://www.nsidc.org/arcticseaicenews/

page 15 *Arctic Code downgraded:* International Maritime Organization, "Guidelines for ships operating in Arctic ice-covered waters," adopted December 23, 2002, available at: http://www.imo.org/includes/blastDataOnly .asp/data_id%3D6629/1056-MEPC-Circ399.pdf

page 15 *the IMO may create standards:* Rob Huebert, "The shipping news part II: How Canada's Arctic sovereignty is on thinning ice," (Summer 2003), 58, *International Journal*, 295 at 300.

page 15 *the most significant threat:* Arctic Council, "Arctic Marine Shipping Assessment 2009 Report," available at: http://arctic-council.org/filearchive/ amsa2009report.pdf

page 17 *terrorist groups might use the Northwest Passage:* Jim Brown, Canadian Press, "Ex-U.S. envoy backs Canada's Arctic claim," *Toronto Star*, August 20, 2007.

page 20 *notions about the Northwest Passage:* Franklyn Griffiths, "Arctic author-ity at stake," *Globe and Mail*, June 13, 1985.

CHAPTER 2: WHO OWNS HANS ISLAND?

page 24 *the Danish claim to Hans Island:* Poul E.D. Kristensen, Ambassador of Denmark, Letter to the Editor ("Hans Island: Denmark Responds"), *Ottawa Citizen*, July 28, 2005.

page 25 *Greenlandic Inuit:* Tom Høyem, "Mr. Graham, you should have told us you were coming," *Globe and Mail*, July 29, 2005.

page 26 *scared the daylights out of scientists:* Joe Ballantyne, *Sovereignty and Development in the Arctic: Selected Exploration Programs in the 1980s* (Whitehorse: self-published, 2009), 7.

page 27 *Welcome to Canada:* Christopher J. Chipello, "It's time to plant the flag again in the frozen north," *Wall Street Journal*, May 6, 2004.

page 27 *return of the Vikings:* Rob Huebert, "The return of the Vikings," *Globe and Mail*, December 28, 2002.

pages 28–29 *joint statement:* Canada-Denmark Joint Statement on Hans Island, September 19, 2005, New York, available at: http://byers.typepad.com/arctic/canadadenmark-joint-statement-on-hans-island.html

page 29 *we adhere to the protocol:* Randy Boswell, "Hans Island was ours first, Greenland says," *Ottawa Citizen*, May 29, 2008.

page 30 *a symbol of peace:* Tom Høyem, "Mr. Graham, you should have told us you were coming," *Globe and Mail*, July 29, 2005.

page 32 *letter written August 8, 1930:* Exchange of Notes regarding the Recognition by the Norwegian Government of the Sovereignty of His Majesty over the Sverdrup Islands, *Canada Treaty Series* 1930, No. 17, available at: http://byers.typepad.com/arctic/1930.html

pages 32–33 *with reference to my note of today:* Ibid.

pages 33–34 *it is the established policy of Canada:* Ibid.

pages 34–35 *the Polar Gas project:* Joe Ballantyne, *Sovereignty and Development in the Arctic: Selected Exploration Programs in the 1980s* (Whitehorse: self-published, 2009), 51.

CHAPTER 3: AN ICE-FREE NORTHWEST PASSAGE

page 36 *the Arctic Grail:* Pierre Berton, *The Arctic Grail: The Quest for the Northwest Passage and the North Pole, 1818–1909* (Toronto: McClelland & Stewart, 1988).

page 38 *Arctic Climate Impact Assessment:* Arctic Council, *Impacts of a Warming Arctic: Arctic Climate Impact Assessment* (Cambridge: Cambridge University Press, 2004), 25.

page 39 *the six lowest maximum events:* David Adam, "Meltdown fear as Arctic ice cover falls to record winter low," *The Guardian*, May 15, 2006.

page 39 *Wieslaw Maslowski warned:* Jonathan Amos, "Arctic summers ice-free 'by 2013,'" BBC News, Dec. 12, 2007, available at: http://news.bbc.co.uk/2/hi/science/nature/7139797.stm

page 39 *longer thaw season/more weakness: From Impacts to Adaptation: Canada in a Changing Climate 2007* (Natural Resources Canada, 2008), 83, available at: http://adaptation.nrcan.gc.ca/assess/2007/index_e.php

page 40 *straight over the top:* Franklyn Griffiths, "Canadian Arctic Sovereignty: Time to Take Yes for an Answer on the Northwest Passage," in Frances Abele et al. (eds.), *Northern Exposure: Peoples, Powers and Prospects in Canada's North* (Montreal: Institute for Research on Public Policy, 2009), 1 at 14–15.

page 43 *Pearson claim over water:* Lester B. Pearson, "Canada Looks Down North" (1946), 24, *Foreign Affairs*, 638 at 639.

page 43 *in no way based on sector principle:* Exchange of Notes regarding the Recognition by the Norwegian Government of the Sovereignty of His Majesty over the Sverdrup Islands, *Canada Treaty Series* 1930, No. 17, available at: http://byers.typepad.com/arctic/1930.html

page 44 *I am here today:* "Securing Canadian Sovereignty in the Arctic," Speech by Prime Minister Stephen Harper, August 12, 2006, Iqaluit, Nunavut, available at: http://byers.typepad.com/arctic/2009/03/securing-canadian-sovereignty-in-the-arctic.html

page 45 *no intention of staking a claim:* Jay Walz, "Oil stirs concern over Northwest Passage jurisdiction," *New York Times*, March 15, 1969.

page 45 *it had to go through territorial waters:* Donat Pharand, "The Arctic Waters and the Northwest Passage: A Final Revisit" (2007), 38, *Ocean Development and International Law*, 3 at 38.

page 45 *the* Manhattan *incident:* I am indebted to Justin Nankivell, my former student and now associate professor at the Asia Pacific Centre for Security Studies, for his doctoral research into this important period in Canadian diplomacy.

page 46 *Arctic Waters Pollution Prevention Act:* Arctic Waters Pollution Prevention Act, Revised Statutes of Canada, 1985, chapter A-12, available at: http://laws.justice.gc.ca/en/A-12/

pages 46–47 *U.S. diplomatic protest:* Press Release No. 121, April 15, 1970, reproduced in (May 11, 1970), 62, *Department of State Bulletin*, 610–11.

page 47 *a drawer full of protests:* Erik Wang, Director of Legal Operations, Department of External Affairs, in *Proceedings of the House of Commons Standing Committee on External Affairs and National Defence*, No. 16, April 27, 1978, at 16.

page 47 UN *Convention on the Law of the Sea:* 1982 United Nations Convention on the Law of the Sea, available at: http://www.un.org/Depts/los/convention_agreements/texts/unclos/closindx.htm

page 50 *a fatal flaw in Canada's argument:* Donat Pharand, *Canada's Arctic Waters in International Law* (Cambridge: Cambridge University Press, 1988), 121–5.

page 50 *Inuktitut place names:* Inuit Place Names Program, at: http://www.ihti.ca/place-names/pn-agreementform.html

page 51 *an exercise of navigational rights and freedoms:* "Department of State telegram 151842, May 17, 1985," reproduced in part in Robert W. Smith and J. Ashley Roach, "Limits in the Seas, No. 112—United States Responses to Excessive National Maritime Claims," (March 9, 1992), available at: http://www.state.gov/documents/organization/58381.pdf

page 51 *agree to disagree:* "Démarche from the United States to Canada, May 21, 1985," reproduced in ibid.

page 51 *committed to facilitating navigation:* "Note from Canada to the United States, dated June 11, 1985," reproduced in ibid.

page 51 *an acceptable arrangement:* Rob Huebert, *Steel, Ice and Decision-Making: The Voyage of the Polar Sea and Its Aftermath* (Unpublished PhD thesis, Dalhousie University, 1994), 239.

page 51 *public anxiety* "Chapter 10—A Northern Dimension for Canada's Foreign Policy," in *Independence and Internationalism: Report of the Special Joint*

Committee of the Senate and of the House of Commons on Canada's International Relations (Ottawa: Queen's Printer, 1986), 127, available at: http://www.carc.org/pubs/v14n04/6.htm

page 51 *Griffiths led the charge:* Franklyn Griffiths, "Arctic authority at stake," *Globe and Mail*, June 13, 1985.

pages 51–52 *Canadian diplomatic note:* "Note from Canada to the United States, dated 31 July 1985," reproduced in Robert W. Smith and J. Ashley Roach, "Limits in the Seas, No. 112—United States Responses to Excessive National Maritime Claims," (March 9, 1992), p. 74, available at: http://www.state.gov/documents/organization/58381.pdf

page 52 *use it or lose it:* Canadian Press, "Use Arctic or lose it, professor tells panel," *Globe and Mail*, July 30, 1985.

page 52 *surprise and disappointment:* "Northwest Passage not for the Soviets, U.S. envoy feels," *Globe and Mail*, August 2, 1985.

page 52 *straight baselines:* Secretary of State for External Affairs the Rt. Hon Joe Clark, Statement in the House of Commons, September 10, 1985, reproduced in Franklyn Griffiths (ed.), *Politics of the Northwest Passage* (McGill-Queen's University Press, 1987), 269 at 271.

page 52 *1951 International Court of Justice decision: Fisheries Case (United Kingdom v. Norway)*, [1951], *International Court of Justice Reports*, 116.

page 53 *Canada's sovereignty is indivisible:* Secretary of State for External Affairs the Rt. Hon Joe Clark, Statement in the House of Commons, September 10, 1985, reproduced in Franklyn Griffiths (ed.), *Politics of the Northwest Passage* (McGill-Queen's University Press, 1987), 269 at 270.

page 53 *1975 Western Sahara judgement: Western Sahara Case (Advisory Opinion)*, [1975], International Court of Justice Reports, 12.

page 53 *paragraph advanced by Inuit negotiators:* 1993 Nunavut Land Claims Agreement, available at: http://www.tunngavik.com/category/publications/nunavut-land-claims-agreement/

page 53 *U.S. diplomatic note:* State Department File No. P86 0019-8641, reproduced in Robert W. Smith and J. Ashley Roach, "Limits in the Seas, No. 112—United

States Responses to Excessive National Maritime Claims," (March 9, 1992), 29, available at: http://www.state.gov/documents/organization/58381.pdf

page 54 *1951 Anglo-Norwegian Fisheries Case: Fisheries Case (United Kingdom v. Norway)*, [1951], *International Court of Justice Reports*, 116 at 142.

page 54 *1949 Corfu Channel Case: Corfu Channel Case (United Kingdom v. Albania)* [1949], *International Court of Justice Reports*, 4 at 28.

pages 54–55 *proof must be adduced:* Donat Pharand, "The Arctic Waters and the Northwest Passage: A Final Revisit," (2007), 38, *Ocean Development and International Law*, 3 at 35 (emphasis in original).

page 55 *Baxter on international waterways:* Richard R. Baxter, *The Law of International Waterways* (Cambridge: Harvard University Press, 1964), 3.

page 55 *some nations take the view:* Richard J. Grunawalt, "United States Policy on International Straits," (1987), 18, *Ocean Development and International Law*, 455 at 456.

page 55 *the test is geographic:* James C. Kraska, "The Law of the Sea Convention and the Northwest Passage," in Brian MacDonald (ed.), *Defence Requirements for Canada's Arctic—Vimy Paper 2007* (The Conference of Defence Associations Institute, 2007), available at: http://www.cda-cdai.ca/cdai/uploads/cdai/2008/12/vimy_paper2.pdf

page 55 *only sixty-nine transits:* Donat Pharand, "The Arctic Waters and the Northwest Passage: A Final Revisit," (2007), 38, *Ocean Development and International Law*, 3 at 38.

page 56 *Ron, that's ours:* Brian Mulroney, "A Call for a New Northern Vision," (June 2006), 27(5), *Policy Options*, 5 at 9.

pages 56–57 *U.S. pledge:* Agreement between the Government of Canada and the Government of the United States of America on Arctic Cooperation, *Canada Treaty Series* 1988, No. 29, available at: http://www.treaty-accord.gc.ca/ViewTreaty.asp?Treaty_ID=101701

page 57 *mandate from the Canadian people:* Gloria Galloway, "Harper rebukes U.S. envoy over Arctic dispute; Ambassador reminded panel that U.S. doesn't recognize Canada's sovereignty," *Globe and Mail*, January 27, 2006.

page 58 *for the record:* Letter from David Wilkins, Ambassador of the United States of America, to Peter Boehm, Assistant Deputy Minister, North America, Department of Foreign Affairs and International Trade, October 27, 2006, available at: www.state.gov/documents/organization/98836.pdf

CHAPTER 4: THE NORTHWEST PASSAGE IN CONTEMPORARY POLICY

page 60 *a listening device off Skull Point:* Joe Ballantyne, *Sovereignty and Development in the Arctic: Selected Exploration Programs in the 1980s* (Whitehorse: self-published, 2009), 8.

page 60 *Northern Watch Technology Demonstration:* Northern Watch Technology Demonstration, Project Overview, at: http://www.ottawa.drdc-rddc.gc.ca/html/project_overview-eng.html

page 60 *Arctic Capabilities Study:* Canadian Directorate of Defence, "Arctic Capabilities Study," in *Final Report—Naval Operations in an Ice-free Arctic Symposium*, April 17–18, 2001, U.S. National Ice Center, available at: http://www.natice.noaa.gov/icefree/Arctic%20Study%20Final%20-%20Canada1.pdf

page 60 *Proliferation Security Initiative:* See: U.S. State Department PSI homepage, http://www.state.gov/t/isn/c10390.htm ; and Michael Byers, "Policing the High Seas: The Proliferation Security Initiative," (2004), 98, *American Journal of International Law*, 526.

page 61 *the coastal state may adopt laws:* Article 42, 1982 United Nations Convention on the Law of the Sea, available at: http://www.un.org/Depts/los/convention_agreements/texts/unclos/closindx.htm

page 62 *functions of bilateral defence command expanded:* Agreement between the Government of Canada and the Government of the United States of America on the North American Aerospace Defense Command, E105060, April 28, 2006, available at: http://www.treaty-accord.gc.ca/ViewTreaty.asp?Treaty_ID=105060

page 63 *O'Connor rose on a point of order:* See: *Hansard*, Vol. 141, No. 16, 1st Session, 39th Parliament, May 4, 2006, 14:55; and *Hansard*, Vol. 141, No. 18, 1st Session, 39th Parliament, May 8, 2006, 15:00.

page 63 *letter of intent phase delayed:* Murray Brewster, "Navy waters down plans for Arctic patrol ships," Canadian Press, June 16, 2009.

page 67 RADARSAT-2 *sale announced, then blocked:* For a longer account, see: Michael Byers, "For Sale: Arctic Sovereignty?" (June 2008), *The Walrus*, available at: http://www.walrusmagazine.com/articles/2008.06-technology-for-sale-arctic-sovereignty-radarsat-mda-michael-byers/

page 67 *Industry Canada blocks purchase of C-27J Spartans:* "Defence Department under fire over $3B plane contract," CBC News, June 9, 2009, available at: http://www.cbc.ca/canada/story/2009/06/09/defence-plane-contract09.html ; for Defence Minister Peter MacKay's response, see: "MacKay defends military's role in $3B plane deal," CBC News, June 10, 2009, available at: http://www.cbc.ca/canada/story/2009/06/10/mackay-plane010.html

page 71 *officials knew nothing about them: Rising to the Arctic Challenge: Report on the Canadian Coast Guard* (Ottawa: Standing Senate Committee on Fisheries and Oceans, April 2009), 58, available at: http://www.parl.gc.ca/40/2/parlbus/commbus/senate/Com-e/fish-e/rep-e/rep02may09-e.pdf

page 71 *Canada does not know as much as it should:* Franklyn Griffiths, "The Shipping News: Canada's Arctic Sovereignty Not on Thinning Ice," (Spring 2003), 58, *International Journal*, 257 at 272.

page 71 *no particular power play:* Andrew Mayeda, "New Arctic protection rules could be tough sell abroad: Harper," *Ottawa Citizen*, August 27, 2008.

page 72 *we will be discussing the proposal with Canada:* CanWest News Service, "U.S. concerned with new Canadian shipping rules in Arctic," *Ottawa Citizen*, August 28, 2008.

page 72 *compulsory reporting not a restriction:* Stuart Kaye, "Regulation of Navigation in the Torres Strait: Law of the Sea Issues," in Donald R. Rothwell and Sam Bateman (eds.), *Navigational Rights and Freedoms and the New Law of the Sea* (Dordrecht: Martinus Nijhoff, 2000), 119 at 127.

page 73 *conservation area studied in Lancaster Sound:* See "Health of the Oceans Initiatives: A Listing by Lead Department or Agency," at: http://www.dfo-mpo.gc.ca/oceans/management-gestion/healthyoceans-santedesoceans/initiatives-eng.htm#natmarine

page 74 *Ice Exercise 2009:* Tony Perry, "Arctic-bound submarine slips out of San Diego," *Los Angeles Times*, February 28, 2009. (The report inaccurately identified the homeport of the *Annapolis* as Norfolk, Virginia).

page 76 *we have a number of bilateral agreements with the U.S.:* Terry Fenge, Letter to the Editor ("Submarines and Arctic sovereignty"), *Globe and Mail*, February 10, 1996.

pages 76–77 *Collenette corrected his statement:* Ibid.

page 77 *the U.S. would have told us:* Jane Taber, "Harper breaks ice on Arctic sovereignty," *Globe and Mail*, December 23, 2005.

page 77 *voyages by U.S. Coastguard icebreakers without prejudice:* Agreement between the Government of Canada and the Government of the United States of America on Arctic Cooperation, *Canada Treaty Series* 1988, No. 29, available at: http://www.treaty-accord.gc.ca/ViewTreaty.asp?Treaty_ID=101701

page 78 *Trudeau declared in 1969:* Hansard, October 24, 1969, at 39.

page 80 *looking at everything through the terrorism prism:* Greg Younger-Lewis, "U.S. might be safer if it left Northwest Passage to Canada: U.S. ambassador," Canadian Press NewsWire, October 7, 2004.

page 80 *Cellucci asked State Department to re-examine position:* "Online Dialogue with Ambassador Cellucci," March 9, 2005, U.S. Embassy "North of Sixty" website, at: http://www.canadanorth.usvpp.gov/yukon/chat.asp (Cellucci wrote: "I have asked people at the State Department to take a look at this, particularly because we do live in the age of the terrorist threat. So it's not a decision for me to make but I have recommended that we take a serious look at our longstanding policy.")

page 80 *Cellucci made his personal views clear:* Daniel LeBlanc, "U.S. reasserts its position on Northwest Passage," *Globe and Mail*, November 1, 2006. Cellucci repeated the point on August 19, 2007, in an interview with CTV's *Question Period*. "I think, in the age of terrorism, it's in our security interests that the Northwest Passage be considered part of Canada," he said. "That would enable the Canadian navy to intercept and board vessels in the Northwest Passage to make sure they're not trying to bring weapons of mass destruction into North America." Jim Brown,

Canadian Press, "Ex-U.S. envoy backs Canada's Arctic claim," *Toronto Star*, August 20, 2007.

page 80 *Pharand told the Standing Senate Committee: Rising to the Arctic Challenge: Report on the Canadian Coast Guard* (Ottawa: Standing Senate Committee on Fisheries and Oceans, April 2009) 27, available at: http://www.parl.gc.ca/40/2/parlbus/commbus/senate/Com-e/fish-e/rep-e/rep02may09-e.pdf

page 81 *pick a fight with the U.S. Navy:* Franklyn Griffiths, "Our Arctic sovereignty is well in hand," *Globe and Mail*, November 8, 2006.

page 82 *U.S. position on transit passage:* Robert W. Smith and J. Ashley Roach, "Limits in the Seas, No. 112—United States Responses to Excessive National Maritime Claims" (March 9, 1992), p. 65, available at: http://www.state.gov/documents/organization/58381.pdf

page 83 *Mary George's analysis of transit passage:* Mary George, "The Regulation of Maritime Traffic in Straits Used for International Navigation," in Alex G. Oude Elferink and Donald R. Rothwell (eds.), *Oceans Management in the 21st Century: Institutional Frameworks and Responses* (Dordrecht: Martinus Nijhoff, 2004), 19 at 38.

page 83 *Harper told Bush about Cellucci's views:* Tonda MacCharles and Bruce Campion-Smith, "Troops out by '09, Bush told," *Toronto Star*, August 21, 2007; Agence France Presse, "No US-Canada thaw on Arctic: officials," August 20, 2007.

CHAPTER 6: WHO OWNS THE SEABED?

page 88 *this isn't the fifteenth century:* Unnati Gandhi and Alan Freeman, "Russian mini-subs plant flag at North Pole sea bed," *Globe and Mail*, August 2, 2007.

page 89 *the Ilulissat Declaration:* "The Ilulissat Declaration," Arctic Ocean Conference, Ilulissat, Greenland, May 27–29, 2008, available at: http://byers.typepad.com/arctic/ilulissat-declaration-may-28-2008.html

page 89 *no race to the North Pole:* Andrew C. Revkin, "5 Countries Agree to Talk, Not Compete, Over the Arctic," *New York Times*, May 29, 2008.

page 89 *oil and gas reserves in the Arctic:* Donald L. Gautier et al., "Assessment of Undiscovered Oil and Gas in the Arctic," (May 29, 2009), 324 (5931), *Science*, 1175–79.

page 90 UN *Convention on the Law of the Sea:* 1982 United Nations Convention on the Law of the Sea, available at: http://www.un.org/Depts/los/convention_agreements/texts/unclos/closindx.htm

page 94 *we're making a claim for posterity:* Jeff Sallot, "Canada joins with Denmark to map depths of the Arctic," *Globe and Mail*, March 24, 2006.

page 95 *our case looks very promising:* Randy Boswell, "'Astonishing' data boost Arctic claim," *Ottawa Citizen*, November 12, 2008.

page 96 *suspicion about Canada's methods and motives:* This section draws on an op-ed co-authored with Ron Macnab, formerly of the Canadian Geological Survey and Canadian Polar Commission: Michael Byers & Ron Macnab, "Show us what lies on the Arctic seabed," *Ottawa Citizen*, May 1, 2009.

page 97 *Harper and Zubkov signed an agreement:* "Joint Statement on Canada-Russia Economic Cooperation," November 28–29, 2007, available at: http://www.international.gc.ca/commerce/zubkov/joint_state-en.asp

page 97 *a joint Russian-Canadian-Danish submission:* See: http://byers.typepad.com/arctic/russiacanada-consultations-on-the-legal-status-of-the-arctic.html See also: Randy Boswell, "Russian bomber outrage came after friendly meeting," *Ottawa Citizen*, May 13, 2009.

page 97 *if anything goes wrong:* Randy Boswell, "Arctic mission at risk, chief scientist says," *Ottawa Citizen*, August 9, 2007.

page 99 *the meridian line of the 141st degree:* Great Britain/Russia: Limits of Their Respective Possessions on the North-West Coast of America and the Navigation of the Pacific Ocean, St. Petersburg, February 16, 1825, 75 *Consolidated Treaty Series* 95.

page 100 *update on the 1867 treaty:* US/USSR: Maritime Boundary Agreement, June 1, 1990, 29 *International Legal Materials*, 941.

page 100 *Antinori on the treaty:* Camille M. Antinori, "The Bering Sea: A Maritime Delimitation Dispute between the United States and the Soviet Union," (1987), 18, *Ocean Development and International Law*, 1 at 34.

page 101 *an equitable result in eastern Alaska:* Ted McDorman, *Salt Water Neighbors: International Ocean Law Relations between the United States and Canada* (New York: Oxford University Press, 2009), 187.

page 101 *a moratorium on exploration:* David H. Gray, "Canada's Unresolved Maritime Boundaries," (Autumn 1997), 5(3), IBRU *Boundary and Security Bulletin,* 61 at 63, available at: http://www.dur.ac.uk/resources/ibru/publications/full/bsb5-3_gray.pdf

page 103 *the predictability that oil companies need:* "Norway and Iceland sign border treaty," *BarentsObserver.com,* November 5, 2008, available at: http://www.barentsobserver.com/index.php?id=4524106&xxforceredir=1&noredir=1

page 103 *as McDorman explains:* Ted McDorman, *Salt Water Neighbors: International Ocean Law Relations between the United States and Canada* (New York: Oxford University Press, 2009), 188.

page 103 *the Inuvialuit Final Agreement:* 1984 Inuvialuit Final Agreement, available at: http://www.irc.inuvialuit.com/publications/pdf/Inuvialuit%20Final%20Agreement.pdf

page 104 *Norway and Russia about to agree on a trade:* "Norwegian-Russian swap deal in the Barents Sea?" *BarentsObserver.com,* September 25, 2008, available at: http://www.barentsobserver.com/index.php?id=4513035&xxforceredir=1&noredir=1

page 104 *Norway's 1930 recognition of Canada sovereignty:* See: Thorleif Tobias Thorleifsson, *Norway "must really drop their absurd claims such as that to the Otto Sverdrup Islands." Bi-Polar International Diplomacy: The Sverdrup Islands Question, 1902–1930* (Unpublished MA Thesis, Simon Fraser University, 2006), available at: http://ir.lib.sfu.ca/retrieve/3720/etd2367.pdf

page 104 *a grand compromise: Rising to the Arctic Challenge: Report on the Canadian Coast Guard* (Ottawa: Standing Senate Committee on Fisheries and Oceans, April 2009), 25, available at: http://www.parl.gc.ca/40/2/parlbus/commbus/senate/Com-e/fish-e/rep-e/rep02may09-e.pdf

page 106 *1951 Anglo-Norwegian Fisheries Case: Fisheries Case (United Kingdom v. Norway),* [1951], *International Court of Justice Reports,* 116.

CHAPTER 7: SOVEREIGNTY AND THE INUIT

page 109 *Canada has a choice:* "Harper on Arctic: 'Use it or lose it,'" *Victoria Times Colonist,* July 10, 2007.

page 110 *a real slap in the face:* Jim Bell, "Exiles denied apology," *Nunatsiaq News,* March 15, 1996.

page 110 *the best interests of the Inuit:* Jim Bell, "What are the exiles signing?" *Nunatsiaq News,* March 15, 1996.

page 111 *that's not going to work:* Author's notes, Session of the Standing Senate Committee on Fisheries and Oceans, June 2, 2008, Iqaluit, Nunavut.

page 112 *Canada's sovereignty supported by Inuit use and occupancy:* 1993 *Nunavut Land Claims Agreement,* available at: http://www.tunngavik.com/category/publications/nunavut-land-claims-agreement/

page 113 *Inuit children are starting over:* Thomas Berger, "'The Nunavut Project': Conciliator's Final Report, March 1, 2006," available at: http://www.tunngavik.com/documents/publications/2006-03-01%20Thomas%20Berger%20Final%20Report%20ENG.pdf

page 114 *new federal money disappointing:* "Houses, Arctic research facility among budget goodies for North," CBC News, January 27, 2009, available at: http://www.cbc.ca/technology/story/2009/01/27/budget-north.html

page 115 *a bright tile in the Canadian mosaic:* Thomas Berger, "'The Nunavut Project': Conciliator's Final Report, March 1, 2006," p. xxi, available at: http://www.tunngavik.com/documents/publications/2006-03-01%20Thomas%20Berger%20Final%20Report%20ENG.pdf

page 119 *Kaludjak told the Standing Committee: Rising to the Arctic Challenge: Report on the Canadian Coast Guard* (Ottawa: Standing Senate Committee on Fisheries and Oceans, April 2009), 36, available at: http://www.parl.gc.ca/40/2/parlbus/commbus/senate/Com-e/fish-e/rep-e/rep02may09-e.pdf

page 120 *Inuit's entrance into Confederation:* Author's notes, Session of the Standing Senate Committee on Fisheries and Oceans, June 2, 2008, Iqaluit, Nunavut.

page 120 *ongoing expression of a negotiated partnership:* Terry Fenge, "Inuit and the Nunavut Land Claims Agreement: Supporting Canada's Arctic Sovereignty," (December 2007–January 2008), 29(1), *Policy Options*, 84 at 86.

page 121 *preamble to the Protocol:* Nunavut Lands and Resources Devolution Negotiation Protocol, September 5, 2008, available at: http://byers.typepad.com/arctic/nunavut-lands-and-resources-devolution -negotiation-protocol-sept-5-2008.html

page 122 *a further exercise of Canada's exclusive authority:* Suzanne Lalonde, "An analysis of the impact devolution of jurisdiction over land and marine bed resources to the Government of Nunavut would have on Canada's claim to sovereignty over the waters of the Arctic Archipelago," Legal Opinion prepared for the Government of Nunavut, February 2008 (on file with author).

page 125 *A Circumpolar Inuit Declaration on Sovereignty in the Arctic*, April 2009, available at: http://www.itk.ca/circumpolar-inuit-declaration-arctic-sovereignty

Recommended Websites

Arctic Centre (University of Lapland) <http://www.arcticcentre.org/>
Arctic Council <http://www.arctic-council.org/>
Arctic Institute of North America (University of Calgary) <http://www.arctic
    .ucalgary.ca/>
Canadian Arctic Resources Committee <http://www.carc.org/>
Canadian Circumpolar Institute (University of Alberta) <http://www.uofaweb
    .ualberta.ca/polar/>
Canadian Polar Commission <http://www.polarcom.gc.ca/>
Institute of Arctic Studies (Dartmouth College) <http://dickey.dartmouth.edu/
    content/view/9/17/>
Inuit Circumpolar Council <http://www.inuitcircumpolar.com/>
Inuit Tapiriit Kanatami (Canadian Inuit national organization) <http://www.itk.ca/>
National Snow and Ice Data Center (U.S.) <http://www.nsidc.org/>
Northern Research Forum (Iceland) <http://www.nrf.is/>
Northern Research Institute (Yukon College) <http://www.yukoncollege.yk.ca/nri/>
Norwegian Polar Institute <http://npweb.npolar.no/english>
Nunavut Government <http://www.gov.nu.ca/>
Nunavut Tunngavik Inc. (Inuit Land Claims Organization)
    <http://www.tunngavik.com/>
Scott Polar Research Institute (University of Cambridge) <http://www.spri.cam
    .ac.uk/>
University of the Arctic <http://www.uarctic.org/>
Who Owns the Arctic?: Arctic Sovereignty and International Relations
    (University of British Columbia) <http://byers.typepad.com/arctic/>

Recommended Readings

Limits in the Sea: United States Responses to Excessive National Maritime Claims (March 9, 1992), 112, *Department of State Bulletin*, available at: http://www.state.gov/documents/organization/58381.pdf

Rising to the Arctic Challenge: Report on the Canadian Coast Guard (Ottawa: Standing Senate Committee on Fisheries and Oceans, April 2009), available at: http://www.parl.gc.ca/40/2/parlbus/commbus/senate/Com-e/fish-e/rep-e/repo2may09-e.pdf

Frances Abele and Thierry Rodon, "Inuit Diplomacy in the Global Era: The Strengths of Multilateral Internationalism," (2007), 13(3), *Canadian Foreign Policy*, 45

Joe Ballantyne, *Sovereignty and Development in the Arctic: Selected Exploration Programs in the 1980s* (Whitehorse: self-published, 2009)

Benoît Beauchamp and Rob Huebert, "Canadian Sovereignty Linked to Energy Development in the Arctic," (September 2008), 61(3), *Arctic*, 341–3

Pierre Berton, *The Arctic Grail: The Quest for the Northwest Passage and the North Pole, 1818–1909* (Toronto: McClelland & Stewart, 1988)

Scott G. Borgerson, "Arctic Meltdown: The Economic and Security Implications of Climate Change," (2008), 87(2), *Foreign Affairs*, 63

Michael Byers, *Intent for a Nation: What Is Canada For?* (Vancouver: Douglas & McIntyre, 2007)

Matthew Carnaghan and Allison Goody, "Canadian Arctic Sovereignty," (26 January 2006), Parliamentary Information and Research Service (PRB 05-61E), Library of Parliament, available at: http://www.parl.gc.ca/information/library/PRBpubs/prb0561-e.htm

Ken S. Coates, P. Whitney Lackenbauer, William R. Morrison and Greg
   Poelzer, *Arctic Front: Defending Canada in the Far North* (Toronto:
   Thomas Allen, 2008)
Elizabeth B. Elliot-Meisel, *Arctic Diplomacy: Canada and the United States in
   the Northwest Passage* (New York: Peter Lang, 1998)
Terry Fenge, "Inuit and the Nunavut Land Claims Agreement: Supporting
   Canada's Arctic Sovereignty," (December 2007–January 2008), 29(1),
   Policy Options, 84
Terry Fenge and Tony Penikett, "The Arctic Vacuum in Canada's Foreign
   Policy," (2009), 30(4), *Policy Options*, 65
Sherrill Grace, *Canada and the Idea of North* (Montreal: McGill-Queen's
   University Press, 2001)
Shelagh Grant, *Sovereignty or Security: Government Policy in the Canadian North
   1936–1950* (Vancouver: University of British Columbia Press, 1988)
David H. Gray, "Canada's Unresolved Maritime Boundaries," (Autumn 1997),
   5(3), IBRU *Boundary and Security Bulletin*, 61, available at: http://www.dur
   .ac.uk/resources/ibru/publications/full/bsb5-3_gray.pdf
Franklyn Griffiths (ed.), *Politics of the Northwest Passage* (Kingston & Montreal:
   McGill-Queen's University Press, 1987)
Franklyn Griffiths, "The Shipping News: Canada's Arctic Sovereignty Not on
   Thinning Ice," (2003), 58(2), *International Journal*, 257
Franklyn Griffiths, "Canada's Arctic Interests and Responsibilities," (2008),
   65(4), *Behind the Headlines*
Franklyn Griffiths, "Canadian Arctic Sovereignty: Time to Take Yes for
   an Answer on the Northwest Passage," in Frances Abele et al. (eds.),
   Northern Exposure: Peoples, Powers and Prospects in Canada's North
   (Montreal: Institute for Research on Public Policy, 2009)
Ivan L. Head, "Canadian Claims to Territorial Sovereignty in the Arctic
   Regions," (1963), 9, *McGill Law Journal*, 200
John Honderich, *Arctic Imperative: Is Canada Losing the North?* (Toronto:
   University of Toronto Press, 1987)
Rob Huebert, *Steel, Ice and Decision-Making: The Voyage of the Polar Sea and
   Its Aftermath* (Unpublished PhD thesis, Dalhousie University, 1994)
Rob Huebert, "The Shipping News Part II: How Canada's Sovereignty Is on
   Thinning Ice," (2003), 58(3), *International Journal*, 295
Rob Huebert, "Canadian Arctic Maritime Security," (Summer 2007), 8(2),
   Canadian Military Journal, 9
Rob Huebert, "Canadian Arctic Security: Understanding and Responding
   to the Coming Storm," (Canadian International Council, 2008)
Guy Killaby, "Great Game in a Cold Climate: Canada's Arctic Sovereignty in
   Question," (Winter 2005–06), 6(4), *Canadian Military Journal*, 31

James C. Kraska, "The Law of the Sea Convention and the Northwest Passage," (2007), 22, *International Journal of Marine and Coastal Law*, 257

Adam Lajeunesse, "Sovereignty, Security and the Canadian Nuclear Submarine Program," (Winter 2007–2008), 8(4), *Canadian Military Journal*, 74

Karin L. Lawson, "Delimiting Continental Shelf Boundaries in the Arctic: The United States–Canada Beaufort Sea Boundary," (1981), 22, *Virginia Journal of International Law*, 221

Natalia Loukacheva, *The Arctic Promise: Legal and Political Autonomy of Greenland and Nunavut* (Toronto: University of Toronto Press, 2007)

Ron Macnab, "The Case for Transparency in the Delimitation of the Outer Continental Shelf in Accordance with UNCLOS Article 76," (2004), 35, *Ocean Development and International Law*, 1

Ted McDorman, *Salt Water Neighbors: International Ocean Law Relations between the United States and Canada* (New York: Oxford University Press, 2009)

Donald M. McRae, "Arctic Sovereignty: What Is at Stake?" (2007), 64(1), *Behind the Headlines*

William R. Morrison, *True North: The Yukon and the Northwest Territories* (New York: Oxford University Press, 1998)

Doug Nord, "Looking for the North in North American Foreign Policies: Canada and the United States," (2007), 37, *American Review of Canadian Studies*, 205

Willy Østreng, *Delimitation Arrangements in Arctic Seas* (The Fridtjof Nansen Institute, Study R007-84 (1985))

Donat Pharand, *Arctic Waters in International Law* (Cambridge: Cambridge University Press, 1988)

Donat Pharand, "The Arctic Waters and the Northwest Passage: A Final Revisit," (2007), 38, *Ocean Development and International Law*, 3

Elizabeth Riddell-Dixon, "Canada and Arctic Politics: The Continental Shelf Extension," (2008), 39, *Ocean Development and International Law*, 343

R.R. Roth, "Sovereignty and Jurisdiction over Arctic Waters" (1990), 28, *Alberta Law Review*, 845

Donald R. Rothwell, *The Polar Regions and the Development of International Law* (Cambridge: Cambridge University Press, 1996)

Christopher Stevenson, "Hans Off! The Struggle for Hans Island and the Potential Ramifications for International Border Dispute Resolution," (2007), 30, *Boston College International and Comparative Law Review*, 263

Jacob Verhoef and Dick MacDougall, "Delineating Canada's Continental Shelf According to the United Nations Convention on the Law of the Sea," (2008), 3, *Journal of Ocean Technology*, 1

Oran R. Young, "Governing the Arctic: From Cold War Theatre to Mosaic of Cooperation," (2005), 11, *Global Governance*, 9

Index

Italicized page numbers indicate figures. Page number suffix "a" refers to appendix pages; "n" refers to endnote pages.

Foxe Basin, 13, 36, 127
Franklin, John, 36–37, 49
Frobisher, Martin, 36, 49
Fry, Eric, 25–26

Gazprom, 10
George, Mary, 83
Georgia Strait Reference (1984), 120
Gillis, Michelle, 17–18
Globe and Mail, The, 27, 51–52
Gotlieb, Allan, 46
Graham, Bill, 27, 77
grasshopper effect, 123
Greenland, 22–26, 41, 105–8, 124–25
Griffiths, Franklyn, 19, 20, 40–41,
    51–52, 71, 81
Grise Fiord (Auyuittuq), 9, *31,* 61, 109
Gulf of Maine Case (1984), 102, 103

Hanseatic, 68
Hans Island, 6, 22–31, *23,* 89, 108, 129
Harper, Stephen: Arctic search-and-
    rescue operations, 67–70; Arctic
    sovereignty as priority, 20–21, 27,
    62; barb aimed at Wilkins, 57–58;
    failure to consult Inuit, 111;
    funding for icebreaker, 85; on
    mandatory registration of shipping,
    71–73; military emphasis, 18;
    obligations under Nunavut Land
    Claims Agreement, 119–23;
    Pacific Gateway Initiative, 86;
    reaction to airspace "incursion"
    by Russians, 2–4; supported
    upgrade of Churchill, 86; surren-
    dered sector theory, 44; timely use
    of Cellucci's support, 83; updated
    Arctic Waters Pollution Prevention
    Act, 70; use it or lose it policy, 109
Head, Ivan, 45–46
Hearn, Loyola, 118

Helena, USS, 74–75
helicopters, for search and rescue,
    67–70
Hendrik, Hans, 24, 25
High Arctic exiles, 109–11
Hill, Jay, 76
Høyem, Tom, 24–25, 26, 30
Hudson Bay, 49
Huebert, Rob, 15, 27, 28, 51
hunting and trapping, 13–14, 25, 33–34,
    36, 73, 114
Hurtig, Mel, 52

icebreakers: *Amundsen,* 9, 36, 38, 62, 127;
    Arctic Cooperation Agreement,
    56–58, 77, 131a; in Arctic Gateway
    Initiative, 87; of Coast Guard,
    62–65, 69–70; *Diefenbaker,* 63, 64,
    65; *Healy,* 95–96; *John A. Macdonald,*
    45; *Louis S. St. Laurent,* 62, 95–96;
    in model Northwest Passage
    negotiation, 84–85, 145a; *North-
    wind,* 45; *Polar 8,* 62; *Polar Sea,*
    51–52, 56–57
Iceland, Arctic policy, 52, 103
Ilulissat Declaration and summit,
    89, 125
immigration issues, 17–18, 61, 84, 144a
Imperial Oil, 98
Inconvenient Truth, An (Gore), 127
Inter-American Commission on
    Human Rights, 124
interdiction policies: and Article 234,
    82–83; in fictional transit scenario,
    136a, 137a, 139–40a; in model North-
    west Passage negotiation, 84,
    144–45a; personnel requirements, 69
internal waters vs. international strait
    issue: actual vs. potential use for
    international navigation, 54–56;
    Arctic Cooperation Agreement,

56–58; Arctic Waters Pollution Prevention Act, 44–48; Cellucci's position, 80, 83, 138a; historic internal waters argument, 48–51; Inuit occupation, 50–51, 53; mandatory controls, 15; Northwest Passage claim, 7, 15, 42–44, 82, 119–23; *Polar Sea* incident, 51–52; provincial examples, 120–21; security issues, 61, 78–81; straight baselines policy, 52–54; submarines and, 75; usage without consent, 77; Wilkins's statement on, 57

International Court of Justice: *Anglo-Norwegian Fisheries Case*, 52, 54, 106–7; Arctic Waters Pollution Prevention Act, 46, 47–48; in fictional interdiction scenario, 138a, 140a; *Gulf of Maine Case*, 102, 103; on nomadic peoples, 53; on straight baselines policy, 52; *Western Sahara Case*, 53, 112

international law: and Arctic Waters Pollution Prevention Act, 45–48; on boundary disputes, 101; on devolution, 122; on diplomatic protests and sovereignty rights, 26; extended continental shelf claims, 10–11; on internal waters claims, 48, 120; international strait, actual use of, 54–56; on knowledge of submarine transits, 76; protests and new rights, 77–78; on sovereignty, 129; straight baselines policy, 53–54; on territorial rights, 5–6; treaty interpretation, 100; use and occupation requirements, 25, 53; Wilkins's interpretation, 58. *See also* International Court of Justice; UN Convention on the Law of the Sea (UNCLOS, 1982)

International Maritime Organization, 14–16, 72

international straits, legal criteria, 42, 54–56. *See also* internal waters vs. international strait issue

Inuit, 109–26; as Canada's Arctic citizens, 115; Circumpolar Inuit Declaration on Sovereignty in the Arctic, 8; concerns about Lancaster Sound as marine conservation area, 73; confronted ss *Manhattan*, 126; education and language issues, 112–13, 116; employment issues, 112–13; excluded from Ilulissat Declaration and summit, 125–26; on Hans Island, 24–25; health and mental health issues, 110, 114; historic use and occupation of Arctic, 50–51, 53, 119–23; housing issues, 113–14; as hunters, 13–14, 25, 36, 50, 126; in international diplomacy, 123–26; and Nunavut economic development, 115–18; Nunavut Land Claims Agreement, 112–14; relocation to high Arctic, 109–11; rights and interests on Hans Island, 30; threatened by climate change, 13–14

Inuit Circumpolar Council, 123, 125–26

Inuvialuit Final Agreement (1984), 103

Inuvialuit Settlement Region, 103, 114

Investment Canada Act, 34, 67

Iqaluit, 37, 65, 87, 111, 115, 118

Kaludjak, Paul, 112, 119, 121

Kessel, Alan, 97

Kolodkin, Roman, 97

Kraska, J.C., 55

Kripanik, Maria, 13

ALEJANDRA AGUIRRE

MICHAEL BYERS holds the Canada Research Chair in Global Politics and International Law at the University of British Columbia. He has led two projects for ArcticNet, a Canadian government-funded research consortium: the first on the Northwest Passage, the second on competing claims to oil and gas reserves below the Arctic Ocean. He is the author of *War Law* and the Canadian bestseller *Intent for a Nation*.